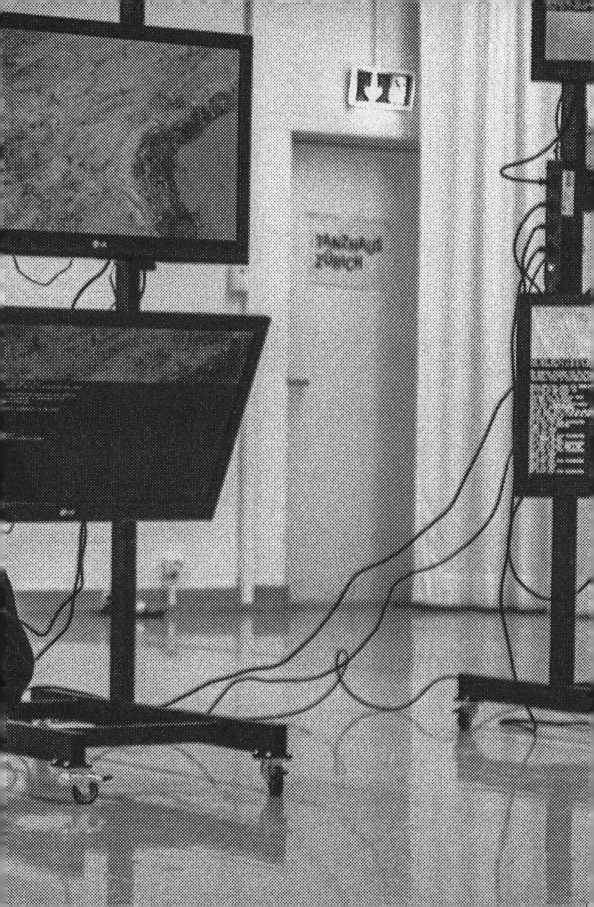

Filming
Researching
Annotating

Research Video
Handbook

Filming
Researching
Annotating

Research Video
Handbook

Editors
Gunter Lösel, Martin Zimper

Birkhäuser
Basel

Contents

Preface and Acknowledgments

We would like to thank all those who have supported us with advice, assistance, and funding, above all the Swiss National Science Foundation (SNSF) and the Zurich University of the Arts. Our heartfelt thanks to Scott deLahunta for providing the initial inspiration and bringing people together, to Florian Dombois for contributing so many ideas at the outset of the project, and to Anton Rey for offering advice when the project encountered crises. We would also like to thank everyone who tested our prototype and gave us feedback, especially the participants at the Research Academy 2018 in Zurich.

It is our hope that with the Research Video project we can contribute to ensuring that artistic research can maintain its proximity to artistic and creative experience. This has been important to us right from the beginning. We have not endeavored to develop an overly theoretical method, but instead have aimed to create a direct approach to generating knowledge that also benefits artists and designers.

The more we approach things with an open mind, the better—that was our guiding principle. Artistic and design research should not be allowed to stray too far from practice; otherwise, it may lose sight of what can make it so valuable.

Zürich 2021

The team of the Research Video project
Gunter Lösel
Martin Zimper
Marisa Godoy
Léa Klaue
Martin Grödl
Moritz Resl
Eric Andreae
Susanne Schumacher
Thomas Schank

Introduction
Gunter Lösel

Can annotated videos serve as a medium for the primary publication of research results? Which new tools, practices, and standards do we need to make it possible? This was the main research question of our project. The present handbook summarizes the results of our research project Research Video, which was executed at the Zurich University of the Arts between 2017 and 2021, led by the Research Focus Performative Practice and the field of study Cast / Audiovisual Media. It was funded by the Swiss National Science Foundation.

We felt–and still feel–that this is an important issue, as certain forms of knowledge and knowledge generation appear to be disadvantaged in the current text-based system for publications. To get a direct impression of the tool and how it works, please visit our website:

www.researchvideo.zhdk.ch

For more than 100 years film and video have been a crucial part of research in various fields like ethnography, sport science, and behavioral sciences, and now increasingly in the field of artistic and design research. With the rise of digitalization and video platforms, they start to unfold their potential as ways to generate new knowledge, share results, and challenge traditional, text-based forms of publication.

Videos are present in every step of research, from video abstracts to data collection, data analysis, interpretation, publication, and the presentation of research. How will this scenario change the way we generate new knowledge? Can a video (or an annotated video) be the sole output of an academic investigation? How will it change the way we share and challenge new knowledge with other researchers and with the public? How can we build up trustworthiness within video-based research and how can we validate it?

Research in fields such as art and design might be at the beginning of a long-term transformation from text-based to enhanced, multimedia practices of publication. The interplay of audiovisual material and language/text has already generated new formats such as video essays or annotated videos and will presumably lead to more formats that will reshape our thinking. Among others they will enable new forms of looking and reflecting on performative practices like theater, dance, and performance art, fostering particular modes of understanding tacit, embodied, and performative knowledges that may help researchers arrive at fresh insights. This calls for new ways of publishing that remix video and text, possibly altering hierarchies, turning video into the primary media and text into the secondary.

Our intention was not only to develop a digital tool, but also to describe the entire research process under the premise that at the end an annotated video would be published. We hypothesized that this would change the way the researchers would think in every preceding phase of research, from the development of the research question to research design, data collection, data analysis, and discussion of results.

1.1 Current State of Research and Discussion

In the artistic research community, the problems of publication have been debated for several years with three main recurring arguments: First, the conventions for scientific publication are generally text-based, which often does not match the modus of artistic thinking and leads to a reduction of possible artistic knowledge generation, especially in the performing arts with its emphasis on embodied knowledge. Second, and related, is the difficulty in maintaining the aesthetic experience throughout the research process, which also influences the role of possible artistic output. Third, not all academic conventions in the human-ities and the social sciences seem to be suitable for a transfer to artistic research without being harmful to its specific form of knowledge generation. There is a growing consensus, however, that some academic conventions are applicable, in particular the criteria of shareability and challengeability (→ see Chap. 8).

Publication Platforms

Publishers are slowly catching on to the trend by accepting video articles: for example, Elsevier and several journals accept video contributions. JoVE (Journal of Visual Experiments) claims to be "the world-leading producer and provider of science videos with the mission to improve scientific research and education" with more than 10,000 videos available. It is not a journal in a classic sense, but rather a repository, and it offers no peer review.

The platform Latest Thinking gets much closer to being a journal, as it proposes a format called "Academic Video" and presents research in a structured way with chapters analogous to a research paper, following the IMRaD Model: Introduction, Method, Results, and Discussion.

The Journal of Embodied Research claims to be "the first peer-reviewed, open access, academic journal to focus specifically on the innovation and dissemination of embodied knowledge through the medium of video." It relies on the format of video essays and provides a peer-review process. The viewer finds the abstract as a text and can view the embedded video essay.

In artistic research two platforms are concerned with developing new formats of publication, the Journal for Artistic Research (JAR) and the Research Catalogue (RC). JAR is published by the Society for Artistic Research (SAR). It is an international, online, open access and peer-reviewed journal for the publication and dissemination of artistic research and its methodologies from all arts disciplines, with the aim of displaying results in a manner that respects artists' modes of presentation. JAR abandons the traditional journal article format and offers its contributors a dynamic online canvas where text can be woven together with image, audio, and video. These research documents, called expositions, provide a unique reading experience while fulfilling the expectations of scholarly dissemination. The journal is underpinned by the Research Catalogue, a searchable documentary database of artistic research. The Research Catalogue reflects a very open conception. Anyone can compose an exposition and add it to the RC using the online editor; suitable expositions can be submitted to the editorial board for peer review and publication in JAR. It is an online database that has been developed as a space for the public storage and exposition of artistic research without submission to outside criteria.

1.2 Our Research Journey and This Book

The project was quite a long journey guided by these questions:

01 If we had a video annotation tool that is optimized for the publication of artistic research, what would it look like?
02 If this form of publication were the primary output of a research project, how would it transform the research process?
03 Could we change the hierarchy of forms of knowledge and come up with a form of research that is more sensitive to embodied knowledge?

In answer to the first question, we have developed the prototype Research Video, which we describe in Chapter 2. The second question concerns the entire research process, and we have devised a general model of the research process that serves as a map to look at the different phases and the use of annotations therein.

This model displays the research process as a sequence of transformed data (→ fig. 01). The original event (e.g. a performance) is transformed into a document (e.g., a video), which is transformed into a corpus of enriched data. Through analysis this big corpus is transformed into a selected corpus of reduced data, which then is the basis for the last transformation into a format of publication. Looking at the research process this way allowed us to be agnostic as to specific traditions of research: no matter what kind of data the research is dealing with, the underlying process stays the same. It also allowed us to trace back the impact of the anticipated output on every step of the transformation process.

There are (at least) four transformations to be made (T1, T2, T3, T4) and we identified the according practices (→ fig. 02). We later added a fifth practice as it proved to be important in the use cases. Getting access to the field can be a crucial first step of research and requires a lot of sensibility and time.

This book will roughly follow this sequence of practices in the model. Chapter 3 addresses with field access, Chapter 4 describes basic practices of video capture, and Chapter 5 covers important aspects of video editing. In Chapter 6 we present and discuss the practices of analyzing and reducing data and finally in Chapters 7, 8, and 9 we take a look at practices that lead to publication. In each of these chapters, we describe our solutions as found in applying the Research Video tool in the use cases.

From Reader to Viewer?

How will a person consume a Research Video? Of course, they will not be in the traditional role of a reader. On the other hand, they will not simply play the video as in a film performance. In fact the misunderstanding we most often encountered with the Research Video is the idea that the additional written information would display synchronously with the video, similar to subtitles. However, the amount of information necessary for scientific depth makes this impossible in principle, in our opinion. Reading or viewing the Research Video must therefore be thought of as a constant alternation between watching the video and reading the annotations.

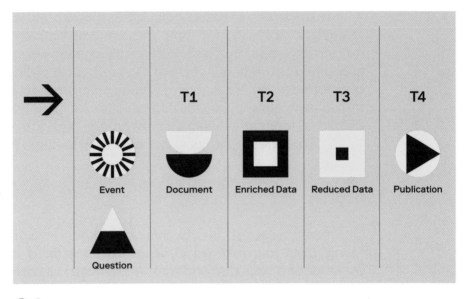

01

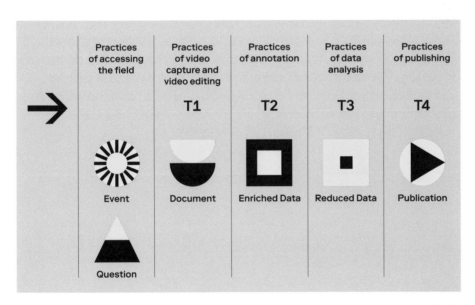

02

Fig. 01:
The research process as a sequence
of transforming data
(illustration by author)

Fig. 02:
The research process as a sequence
of practices to transform data
(illustration by author)

The practice of reading becomes a new practice of reading-viewing, which is somewhere in the middle between playing a video and reading a text. If annotated videos become a new standard for the publication of research, they will have to find a balance between reading and viewing. One important observation is that, compared to video essays and documentaries, the control of reading-viewing shifts from the author to the reader-viewer, who will create his or her own path through the material.

Detours

Like most research projects, this one has not developed in a linear fashion, but has involved some detours and dead ends. There was a lot of discussion and wishful thinking that could not be put into practice. We therefore decided to dedicate a separate chapter, Chapter 10, to ideas and goals that arose during the project but could not be realized. This includes the identified needs for easier usability and easier permanent storage.

A specific problem we faced was the discovery that it proved impossible–or beyond our capacities–to edit video material after it had been annotated without losing the position of the annotation. We could not accept this at first, so we started an additional project called Sticky Annotations, which shows different technical solutions and analyzes their effort and risks. You can find the report of this subproject here:

https://docs.google.com/
document/d/1iSm3hNYGaZ9XVQcmHiGYuhSb9p2Eb6XRaSXiLMI3hrY/edit

We were not able to solve this problem within the framework of this project, but we are convinced that it will be solved eventually and that our report will contribute to this.

Apart from this dead end, we did arrive at satisfying and encouraging results: a usable tool, multiple use cases, a practicable workflow, and a concrete vision for the publication of annotated videos as research outputs. To our great pleasure, the Research Catalogue agreed to install a gateway so that Research Video projects can be published both in the Media Archive of the Zurich University of the Arts and in the Research Catalogue. We hope that researchers from various disciplines will take up the topic of annotated videos in their research and that our preliminary work can be of use in this context.

Our intention was not only to
also to describe the entire
premise that at the end an
published. We hypothesize
way the researchers would t
of research, from the devel
tion to research design, dat
and discussion of results.

evelop a digital tool, but
earch process under the
notated video would be
at this would change the
k in every preceding phase
nent of the research ques-
ollection, data analysis,

A New Tool:
Research Video
Martin Grödl, Moritz Resl

We briefly describe how the Research Video application was created, focusing in particular on assumptions, guiding principles, and design decisions. The premise was that video could be a central medium of a new form of publication, dubbed "enhanced publication." Based on this premise, the goal was to create methods and tools for artistic and process-bound research. If possible, it would use and build upon established standards for scientific publications like the IMRaD publication structure ⟨Intro, Methods, Results, and Discussion⟩, references, citability, shareability, and challengeability of research results.

Since it was established that annotated video would be the main medium of the project, we conducted a cursory investigation of other major use cases of annotated video: film (subtitles, transcription), linguistics (phonetics, gestures), anthropology/ethnology ("coding"), and computer vision (automated segmentation).

Next we looked at "prior art," that is, existing video annotation software. We tested seven applications in total, including ELAN and ANVIL, each with the same simple use case of opening a short video file and annotating a certain region. We took note of a number of important observations, which allowed us to formulate our own goals more clearly.

Guiding Observations in the Development Process

○ Technical restrictions
Most of the tools were hard to even get running due to technical restrictions like operating system requirements or dependencies on other software or libraries.

○ Unsupported/outdated systems
Some were based on closed or unsupported/outdated systems like Flash.

○ Lack of support
Video format support was generally lacking.

○ Made for experts
Most of the tools were focused on certain use cases, like transcription or linguistics, and made by experts in the respective fields for use by other experts.

○ Subpar user experience
In general, user experience was subpar. User interfaces were laggy and unresponsive, and conventional keyboard shortcuts (for example for play/pause, copy/paste) were often unsupported.

○ Difficult to get started
It was surprisingly difficult to get started using those programs, even with our minimal use case. In many situations it was impossible to complete the task intuitively, without studying the user manuals.

2.1 Design Decisions

Based on this research we identified a number of core concepts common to many annotation tools as well as video editing software. To facilitate communication within the project team we agreed to consistently use certain terms for these concepts. This resulted in the following nomenclature.

Terms for Core Concept

○ Timeline (annotation board)
○ Track (tiers, layers)
○ Annotation (marker, interval, element, label)
○ Annotate (coding, labeling, markering, segmentation)
○ Annotation scheme (coding scheme, controlled vocabulary)

Taking into account the findings above, we came to the decision that a fresh take on video annotation was promising, and we formulated our goals.

Goals for the Reasearch Video Tool

○ Easy to use
We found that most current tools are lacking in User Interface Design. Therefore we decided to make a user-centered design and usability by nonexperts our core goals.

○ Easily accessible
As many previous tools present a significant obstacle to users by requiring specific platforms, install procedures, or additional restrictions, we aimed to remove this hurdle by building a tool on web technologies. This meant that our application should run in any current web browser, requiring no install.

○ Open
Being part of a research project, we decided to use open technologies as much as possible as well as an open source development model. The complete source code of the application is open and can be studied, modified, and extended freely.

○ Based on best practices
We decided to put a special emphasis on following well-established conventions regarding user interfaces and the video medium in particular.

In the following we briefly point out a few examples of guiding principles we tried to follow in the design of the Research Video application.

Examples of Guiding Principles

○ Habituation
If something works in a certain way, it is expected to work like that everywhere and always, even across applications. When making use of this principle, the user no longer needs to think consciously about how certain things work. For example, there are commonly used hotkeys, like Spacebar for toggling between play and pause and Backspace for deleting the current selection of elements.

○ Streamlined repetition
Refine common and repetitive tasks first, to make them as simple as possible. In the case of our application, this mainly concerns adding and editing annotations, which forms the core task of Research Video.

○ Instant gratification
Help your users achieve a feeling of success, even if it's just small things. In our case, when somebody starts up the application for the very first time, we immediately give them a working example project to explore and play around with.

In the course of developing the application we adopted two additional principles, mainly due to limitations on development resources, but very helpful nonetheless. Already in the prototype phase of the project we decided not to include any networking component. So even though the application is accessed online, there are no servers hosting video and annotation data. The web is just a delivery mechanism for the application. All the application data is kept locally in the browser's storage and is retained between sessions. Additionally users can export their projects, producing a ZIP file that can be stored or shared with other users.

Obviously this decision saved resources for building and maintaining server components, but it proved especially practical in academic workshop settings, where many users needed to access the application over spotty Wi-Fi connections.

When developing new features in a user interface, there are usually multiple options to enable a certain user action. Often there is no clear better or preferred option; on the contrary, they often are complementary and accommodate different users. Being an experimental project with limited resources, we decided that in most cases it wasn't feasible for us to implement multiple solutions. Thus we chose to adopt as a guideline to provide one solution for one problem, sometimes called the KISS principle. This allowed us to develop features more quickly and gather user feedback before elaborating on the design.

Finally it should be noted that all mentioned design principles are not strict rules, but guidelines. Sometimes they can even be in conflict with each other, so a decision of priority has to be made. Nevertheless these guiding principles provide a valuable and consistent basis to make informed and well-balanced design decisions.

$\mapsto$

2.2 User Interface and Instruction Manual

We'll briefly describe the user interface and its functionality and features. You can watch tutorials on how to use the Research Video tool on the project website:

https://researchvideo.zhdk.ch

User Interface

Browser and Layout	Research Video runs in Google Chrome. The layout of Research Video is divided into four sections (A, B, C D).

A	**Toolbar Component**	Here you can control the most important features with icons.
B	**Video Component**	This is where the video player is located with the selected video file.
C	**Inspector Component**	The Inspector hosts all annotations and serves as a tool for editing annotation data: Start Time, Duration, Title, and Description. A selected annotation (indicated by a frame) can be deleted with the Backspace key.
D	**Timeline Component**	The Timeline hosts all tracks and annotations. Time is represented from left to right. Furthermore, a playhead indicates the current time position within the video file. Annotations are added here; start time and duration can be adjusted by dragging. In this component, tracks can be added, edited, and deleted.

Instruction Manual

Start Research Video	Research Video is developed for Google Chrome. Download it here: → https://www.google.com/chrome. To start the application, visit → https://rv.zhdk.ch.
Load Video/ Change Video File	The first thing you likely want to do is start a <u>project</u>. Open the <u>Project Overlay</u> by selecting the respective button in the <u>Toolbar</u> (A) and select a video file you want to work with. The video file should be in <u>MP4/H.264</u> format.

Video Format Considerations

The best supported video format for the web browser (and therefore video) is:
- MP4 with H.264 Codec
- Recommended resolution 720p30 (1280×720 px, 30 FPS)
- Recommended target bitrate 5 Mbps
- Recommended maximum length: 60 minutes

To export this format from <u>Adobe Premiere</u>, use these settings:
- File → Export Media
- Format: H.264
- Preset: Mobile Device 720p HD

You can convert existing videos using the free tool <u>Handbrake</u>:
- Download: → https://handbrake.fr
- Preset: General → Fast 720p30

Set Title for Project

An arbitrary project title can be set. Saved project files are named after the title. If no title is set, it defaults to "Untitled project." Below a cropped view of Research Video project named "Projektname1."

R_V	Projektname 1

⊕ Add   ⊖ Delete   ⧉ Copy   ⧉ Paste   # Tag   ↶ Undo   ↷ Redo   ■ Project   ☐ Current annotations only

Add/Edit/Delete Annotation	To add an annotation, double-click within a track in the Timeline (D) or select the respective button in the Toolbar (A). A window for the annotation appears in the Inspector (C). To edit an annotation, select it either on the track or directly in the Inspector (C) with a mouse click. A selected annotation is highlighted with a black frame and can be edited in the Inspector (C). Selected annotations can be deleted by pressing the Backspace key or by pressing the respective button in the Toolbar (A).
Add URL to Annotation	The annotation format is minimal (text-only) but allows for linking other resources by pasting a URL into the description of an annotation. This way anything on the web can be attached freely to any annotation.
Add/Edit/Delete Track	Add a track by selecting the respective button in the bottom right corner of the Timeline (D). To delete a track, hover over the track and click the X-symbol in the top right corner. Click the title of a track to edit it.
Hide Track	You can hide or reveal a track by toggling the eye icon at the right side of a single track. Hiding tracks can improve the readability of the project, if you have created many tracks.
Export Project	Open the Project Overlay by selecting the respective button in the Toolbar (A) and select the Export button. Think of exporting a project as a way of saving it. You can also share the file with others. One can simply open the project in the app.
Open Project	Open the Project Overlay by selecting the respective button in the Toolbar (A), then select the Load button. You can now load previously saved *.rv files. To work on more than one project, open another window in your browser.
Reset	Open the Project Overlay by selecting the respective button in the Toolbar (A), then select the Reset button to reset the current project to its template state.
Show Current Annotations Only	A toggle that, when checked, hides all annotations in the Inspector that are not currently under the playhead. Works dynamically, that is, when the project is playing. |→

Search Function	Typing text into the search box starts a live search. The annotations that match the search are displayed in the Inspector. The chronological order of annotations in the Inspector is preserved.

There is a toggle Apply to Timeline, which, when on, also applies the search result to the Timeline. Only annotations that match the search are shown on the Timeline.

Tagging	A Tagging system helps organize, find, and view annotation content.

Within any annotation text, a tag can be added by using the hash character (#) followed by any word. Example: #experimental. This is consistent with the use of hashtags in many well-known web applications (Twitter, YouTube, Instagram, Facebook, etc.). A visual highlight (background color) is applied to tags.

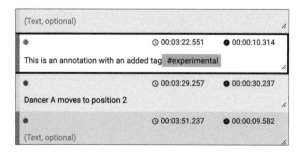

After a #-character is typed, the tagging box opens, which shows a scrollable list of all used tags in this project sorted alphabetically. As you type, the list is filtered dynamically, only showing tags that begin with the typed string. When selecting Space or Enter or selecting one of the suggestions, the tag is added.

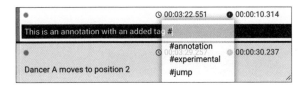

To delete a tag, hover over the tag, and an X-symbol will appear, overlaying the text after the tag. Select the X-symbol to remove the tag.

2.3 Pointer Feature

Spatial position in video can be highlighted by using a pointer. This enables the user to draw attention to specific areas of the screen, thus not only indicating when something of interest occurs but also where. This should be handy in many cases, for example, when multiple dancers, objects, props, etc. are on-screen simultaneously.

In this first iteration, we intentionally limit this feature to indicating a single point in screen space for the entire length of the annotation.

An annotation now consists of start time and duration (both timestamps), a screen location (x and y coordinates), and the annotation content (text).

The pointer extends the annotation data model by introducing an optional x/y-value pair. On an abstract level this means that in addition to referencing a specific time in the video, an annotation can now also reference space. In the context of video, space refers to the two-dimensional image plane of the frame.

Pointer Workflow

Create Pointer

Select the gray dot in the annotation (Inspector view). The dot color in Inspector changes to the respective track color. The pointer appears in the center of the video; and the playhead jumps to the beginning of the annotation.

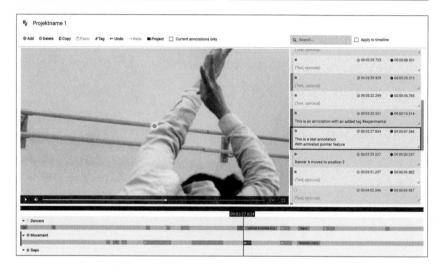

Set X/Y Position

If the annotation is selected (indicated with a black border), the pointer can be dragged. If the pointer is selected (and possibly dragged) in the video, the annotation is also selected.

Delete/Deactivate Pointer

To delete the pointer, hover over the colored dot in the Inspector view. An X-symbol will appear. By selecting the X-symbol, the pointer disappears in all components and the dot color returns to gray.

Pointer Indication in UI

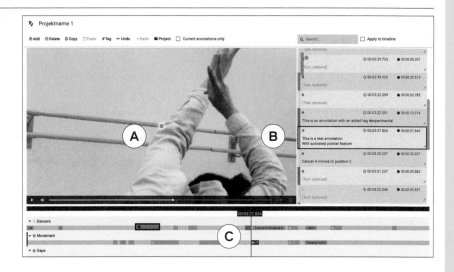

| A | Pointer Representation in Video | Small circular shape, white stroke
If the corresponding annotation is selected: white outer glow |

| B | Pointer Representation in Inspector | Colored dot: active pointer
Gray dot: no pointer |

| C | Pointer Representation in Timeline | Black dot in front on text (if any) |

Chronological Sorting If there's more than one pointer at a given time, sorting should be chronological, that is, the last occurring point is drawn last, and therefore is on top.

Hotkeys

Dbl Click in Timeline	Add new annotation
Backspace	Delete selected annotations
Spacebar	Pause/play video
+ or]	Add new track
Cmd + C	Copy selected annotations
Cmd + V	Paste annotations
Cmd + Z	Undo
Cmd + Shift + Z	Redo

2.4 Technical Information

This section provides some technical information, mainly aimed at developers who want to extend the software.

All code is free software and open source. Development takes place publicly on GitHub, where the latest version of the source code can be viewed and downloaded:

https://github.com/StudioProcess/rvp

The source code is distributed under the GNU General Public License, Version 3. According to this license, anyone is free to use the software for any purpose, change the software for their own needs, and share the software including any changes of their own, provided the changed software is distributed under the same terms. More information including the full text of the license is available online:

https://www.gnu.org/licenses/gpl-3.0.en.html

Core Technologies

The web framework used is Angular. It provides a build system (Angular CLI) as well as a modular component-based architecture for the application:

https://angular.io

For managing the application state we use NgRx. This technology allows us to deal with complex user interactions and their effects on the application state and enables crucial application features like Undo/Redo:

 https://ngrx.io

Core Data Model

The core data type in the application is an annotation. It consists of an ID, so it can be uniquely referenced, a global timestamp (UTC in seconds with fractional part), a duration (seconds with fractional part), and an annotation body called "fields." Currently only a single field called "description" is used, containing a plain text string.

3

Filming People: Reflections on Entering the Field
Léa Klaue

Artistic and applied research videos often focus on people. How do researchers gain access to individuals, artists, or communities? How do they build trust with the subjects of their films? And how can they make their films seem natural and realistic? Problems and solutions for one important step in the research process: working with people in the field.

Video publications often aim for authenticity and legitimacy or strive for an absolute objectivity. Anyone who enthusiastically embraces these ideals should be aware that true objectivity does not exist. Every seemingly objective view presented through the medium of video is a constructed one. Authenticity is a construct of random activities whose aim is to convey a sense of truthfulness.

In their role as filmmakers, researchers gain control of the camera themselves. They decide when something is filmed, when it is not, which shots will be included in the final film, and which shots will not. Anyone who lays claim to being objective in a film must first grapple with themselves and their own perspective. A thorough examination of personal perspectives and ideals, as well as of the origins and traditions of knowledge, is essential to show or "prove" something through the medium of video.

Legitimate researchers document their processes, successes, and failures, so that their research findings can be acknowledged and used by the research community. Filmmaking researchers attach as much importance to the process as to the results. In traditional filmmaking, this is not always the case. Traditional filmmakers and designers usually focus exclusively on the end result: what effect is created by a certain type of lighting? What atmosphere is produced by certain sounds? What impression is being conveyed on-screen by the person being interviewed? Elements of reality are thus introduced and curated instead of simply being filmed as they exist in the real world. Generally speaking, traditional filmmakers attach little importance to the path that leads them to the finished product, and use selected methods simply to get them there. In the process, little or no thought is given to these methods.

Researchers working with video should consider and appreciate all steps in the process. It is often more of an obstacle than an aid to enter a research field with a fixed idea about a final product. The reason is that researchers will then be less open to surprising, unforeseen, and possibly interesting phenomena. The perspective of the goal-oriented artist should not eclipse that of the curious researcher.

For her dissertation, the author of this article is currently pursuing a research video project that is based on participatory video research with independent child workers in Bolivia. Through empirical research, the project aims to highlight the voices of these young subjects. Video is excellently suited for this purpose as it can be used to collect data in a creative and playful way. With the help of video, the author has captured the sensory characteristics of places and situations, which in turn serves the project's ethnographic objectives.

The second dissertation project devoted to Research Video is being implemented by Marisa Godoy, a dancer, choreographer, and dance researcher. Godoy is using audiovisual methods to observe and investigate a form of practiced perception in the joint creative processes of a dance ensemble. The video material and the annotation capabilities of the Research Video tool offer a new way to document, describe, and analyze the intricate, lengthy processes that characterize the creation of improvisational choreography.

3.1 Context Determines Style and Form

The style, format, and genre of a video are determined by the context in which a researcher uses video methods and incorporates other people, research partners, subjects, and fellow researchers into the project.

Anyone wishing to study "everyday" social issues in relation to groups of people in defined places such as school classrooms can take a camera to one of these places and inconspicuously record the normal course of the day in the style of "Observational Cinema". Of course, consent must first be obtained from all of the subjects–in the case of a classroom, from teachers and parents.

If sensitive content must be shown or the identities of people hidden, careful consideration must be given to how the medium of video is used. Filmmakers can disguise voices or conceal faces and even entire locations and landscapes in creative ways through animations, staged scenes with actors, or other fictional elements. In such cases, it is important to document and create legitimacy for the process. To avoid confusing viewers, it must be clear in the video that actors are staging the scene. When addressing sensitive issues, the author of this article used theatrical and cinematic methods to ensure the subjects always felt at ease and did not suddenly withdraw from the project.

01

02

Figs. 01 and 02:
Research participants or protagonists
discuss the scenes to be staged and
shot with the researcher. Screenshot
from the research material
(Léa Klaue, Bolivia 2018)

Assessing Feasibility Realistically

Making a film about a research process can be tempting, but the technical, legal, and financial challenges–as well as the time required–are often underestimated.

Artistic and applied researchers who are not trained in the use of video are often the ones unable to put their ideas into practice as originally intended. Space and time are essential to remain flexible and to be able to improvise. In many cases, costs are also underestimated. Gear is not always cheap, nor is the editing and post-production software. Researchers who do not wish to learn the skills of the trade must factor in the additional cost of hiring specialists who know how to use the software and tools.

Finding Suitable Protagonists

Researchers should start searching for suitable protagonists when developing their research idea. The most important questions are: Are the people in question interesting for my audience? Who exactly is my audience? What do the people I have selected have to do with my research topic? What factors have consciously or unconsciously influenced my selection? Why should "educated" viewers take an interest in my subjects? Is my research topic linked to stereotypical views of others, and if so, how can I combat them?

The selected people will have different motives, motivations, and views. At times, researchers may disagree with their opinions on various levels. They might even dislike these individuals. In such cases, they should be honest about their feelings and attempt to reflect on and clearly understand their own feelings and the feelings of other people involved. As a general rule, researchers do not need to feel sympathy for their subjects, but they should always feel empathy.

3.2 Building Relationships and Trust

Filming people means building relationships with them, and relationships require an investment of time. It can take a long time for subjects to learn to trust researchers, to feel comfortable and open up in front of them and the camera. Building relationships means engaging in long discussions and taking an interest in all aspects of a person's life. It is also important for researchers to be willing to open up to the subjects and make their own lives part of the process. For example, for the author's PhD project with children and young people in Bolivia, it was important for her to discuss her family, friends, childhood, and school, to show photographs and videos, and to tell anecdotes.

Filmmakers must cultivate the communication with research partners and remain attentive to their needs. Discussions should be reflected on in depth.

Obtaining Consent

Sufficient time and attention should be devoted to negotiating the participant's consent for filming. The conditions must be clear and repeated several times. Written contracts can be helpful, but are not always necessary, depending on the place, legal conditions, general situation, and the setup of the shooting.

Who and what will be filmed? Under what conditions? Is the filmmaker/researcher affiliated with a particular institution? Is this institution based in another country? Where and in what context will the video material be published? In many cases and for various reasons, the subjects may not fully understand the content of a contract. Conflicts often arise with subjects after the release of film material, and they sometimes have no means to defend themselves.

It is crucial for researchers to build and maintain trust and be aware of their position and possible (invisible) power relations. The people filmed may consent to the publication of film material in various channels. They must be completely clear on the consequences of giving consent. In many cases, a contract is not enough. The more time and energy that is invested in building trust, the lower the risk of a participant suddenly withdrawing from the project.

Many people are unaware of how widely their images will be distributed on the internet and the dramatic consequences this can have. During the author's first research stay in Bolivia, she met a fourteen-year-old girl who, in addition to participating in her research project, gave an interview with a European public broadcaster. The girl was promised that the interview would only be released in Europe. Four years later, the video had found its way through various social media channels and became known to the Bolivian public. Although it only addressed topics considered harmless by the European journalists, it ultimately caused a major conflict in her family and led to the girl being thrown out of her parents' home and harassed during her studies.

For her field research, Marisa Godoy gave the dancers she planned to observe an information sheet about her research project and a statement of consent for data acquisition. Such contracts can be adapted to the research situation. Godoy used two types of contracts: one for all the dancers who would be visible in the video recordings and one for the people she interviewed. One of the clauses in the contract stipulated that it was impossible to anonymize the research video material, which meant the dancers would be visually recognizable in the video and no measures would be taken to conceal their identity.

At times, though, contracts may be superfluous. In the author's case, for example, no written contracts were used for various ethical reasons. To begin with, some of the protagonists were minors and it would have been necessary to obtain consent from their parents or guardians. This was difficult in the Bolivian context because some parents spoke indigenous languages instead of Spanish, were illiterate, or were absent from their children's lives. The author obtained oral consent from the parents she was able to visit. In addition, all of the young participants in the research project were recorded giving their consent in front of the camera.

Self-Perception

When researchers enter a new setting for the first time, especially as "outsiders", they should try to understand how they are perceived by others. How are they treated, in both a positive and negative sense, as compared to others? Are they in a privileged position that allows them to stand out from the crowd?

It can be helpful to show up with the camera as early as possible in the process. In this way, people can get used to the camera's presence more quickly. It is a shame to spend a lot of time building relationships only to have them damaged or completely destroyed by the sudden, late, or intimidating appearance of the camera (or cameraperson).

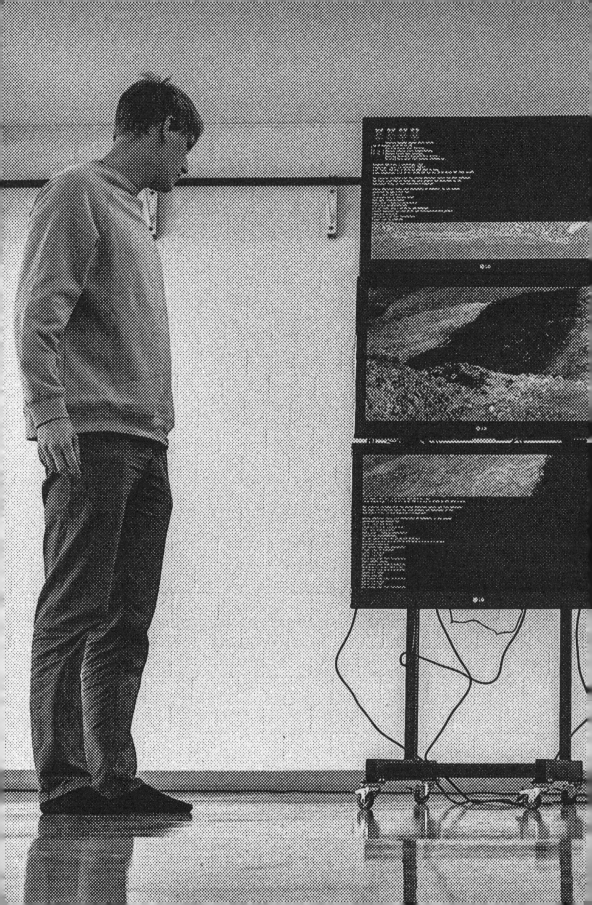

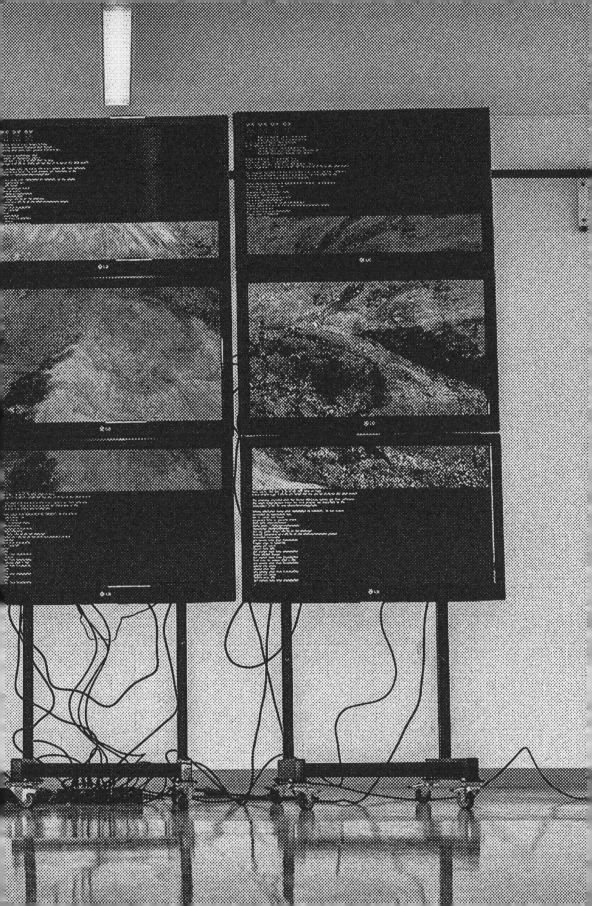

Expectations of the People Being Filmed

The attitudes of the subjects of the film should be evaluated at an early stage in the process. The first step is to understand why they have consented to be filmed. Out of sympathy? Due to specific interests? Or perhaps due to a different reason or a hidden motive? Some people are attracted to the camera and film media and are attention-seekers. In some cases, potential interested parties may go to excessive lengths to adapt to circumstances. They may try to guess what the researchers/filmmakers are looking for and conform to their expectations, perhaps even playing a role. However, this can be disruptive to the research process.

It must be made clear to all participants that the project's aim is not to produce an advertising film and that the research video is not promoting or selling anything. Explaining this can sometimes be a difficult, lengthy process.

3.3   Preparation and Research

Marisa Godoy had experience working behind the camera before she began her research, but she had never used ethnographic methods. In order to get a feel for what it would be like in the field, to gain clarity on her own position, and to learn how to use the camera, she organized a "field research pilot project" before her research began. She visited a dance group during a rehearsal and simulated a research and observational situation with the camera. These types of exercises can help researchers prepare for their field research, choose the most suitable equipment, and become comfortable using it.

It can also be helpful to do some research before the actual shooting, though sometimes too much prior knowledge can hamper the research process. It can awaken certain expectations and cause researchers to focus on certain aspects of the work. As a result, they may forget to take in the entire field and may not respond to unexpected phenomena. One often hears talk of the "curious gaze" of researchers who respond to all events and changes in the field and evaluate everything anew on a daily basis. This may seem counterproductive if the aim is a fixed, planned filming process, but every filmmaking researcher needs to give careful thought to the proper balance between "planned" and "spontaneous."

It was important for Marisa Godoy to bring her skills and knowledge as a dancer to her field research and to position herself as a practice-oriented researcher. Ultimately, it is up to the researchers making the film to decide how they want to position themselves in the field and establish relationships with the people in front of the camera. A high degree of creativity and flexibility will always be necessary.

Researchers working with v
appreciate all steps in the pr
obstacle than an aid to ente
a fixed idea about a final pr
researchers will then be les
unforeseen, and possibly in
perspective of the goal-orie
eclipse that of the curious r

o should consider and
ess. It is often more of an
research field with
uct. The reason is that
pen to surprising,
esting phenomena. The
d artist should not
archer.

Filming Research: Video Recordings
Eric Andreae

Researchers in the performative arts, fine arts, and design, not to mention the social sciences, are usually not trained filmmakers who are skilled at working with a video camera. Nevertheless, they too can shoot high-quality videos. Getting started is easy enough. In many cases, a high-end smartphone is all you need for a research project with moving images. However, every researcher should know and observe a few basic rules of thumb about video recordings, shots, and angles.

A conventional video can be understood as a "show-and-tell": the filmmakers intend to depict something specific and rely on the medium to accomplish that. <u>They understand precisely the objects and narratives that they intend to portray with the camera.</u>

A research video is fundamentally different because the researchers cannot know with certainty what they will find. They are essentially gazing into the unknown. In this context, videos provide a means of gaining new insights when researchers repeatedly view and analyze the recordings later on. The phenomena and patterns that are of relevance to the study are often only discovered during the subsequent research process. Video researchers thus face a paradox. If they point the camera only at what is already known, the video may not produce any insights. If, on the other hand, they point the camera at what is unknown, this raises the question of what should be filmed, since what is new has not yet been revealed at the time of the recording. There are three solutions to this paradox.

Procedure of Filming

01   Clarify the questions
Clarifying the question and clearly establishing the factors to be examined requires a certain amount of prior knowledge about what exactly to expect, as well as where and how the relevant effects will manifest themselves.

02   Record as much as possible
If the researcher does not know if, when, and where effects will occur or what they may look like, virtually the only alternative is to record "everything"–although this immediately raises the question of what "everything" means in each specific situation. A number of video cameras and 360-degree cameras allow for a certain amount of selecting to be made when shooting. However, this produces an enormous amount of data, which can be overwhelming and only properly handled with automation.

03   Proceed intuitively
The exact opposite approach is to be radically selective during the recording process, and to record only phenomena that the researchers suspect may be the key to revealing hidden information. This skill must first be learned, similar to the way a mineral

collector learns to examine a rock to see whether it contains crystals or not. This third method is closely related to artistic research.

Regardless of which of the three approaches is selected, the videos must have a certain degree of quality to be suitable for subsequent evaluation. Researchers therefore require a certain basic level of expertise, which they cannot automatically be assumed to possess.

4.1 Camera Shots

Camera shots are the basic building blocks of filmmaking and video productions. They begin the moment the camera starts rolling and recording images. Unlike a still camera, a video camera can pan, track, and zoom. The shot ends when the camera stops filming. Within a single shot, the time of the filmed reality (action in front of the camera) is synchronous with the playback time (narrative time). Otherwise, real time is generally shortened or sometimes even stretched by "cuts".

Shots only take on meaning when they are arranged as a sequence within a context. The process of interlinking shots obliges the filmmaker to consider transitions and junctions: image sizes, camera positions, angles, movement, and content-related associations between foreground, middle ground, and background have to be viewed and reflected upon over and over again. |→

Shot Sizes and Angles

Extreme wide shots/wide shots/long shots	Best for a vast landscape or a town or village.
Totale	Emphasizes the scenery but includes subjects and/or objects in full view, essentially for orientation. Full shots have to be shown for much longer than wider shots because they usually contain a great deal of detailed information that the viewer needs time to absorb.
The medium long shot	In a medium long shot, there is no longer an emphasis on distance. Only part of a room or landscape is shown. Small groups become visible, for example. However, people can still be seen in their entirety and at full size, that is, for a small screen: facial expressions, gestures, and other subtleties still remain out of focus. This is still a shot that provides an overview.
Cowboy shot	This shot comes straight out of Hollywood westerns and shows actors with their Colt six-shooters visible on their thighs. It is suitable, for example, for capturing an image of a person who is presenting something. In this shot, you still have sufficient scope to react if the filmed object suddenly changes position.
Medium shot	This shows the subject with between half and one-third of their body visible. The camera abandons the position of an impartial observer and becomes selective in its view.
Medium close-up shot	The subject is shown from head to shoulder, and part of the upper body is visible. The emphasis is on the face or on the center of an object, but this shot still conveys the impression of maintaining the perceived personal space around the subject, that is, a distance of approximately an arm's length from the camera.
Close-up shot	In shots of people, a close-up face shot would fill the entire frame. All that can be seen here is the central motif, which the viewer simply cannot miss. The camera focuses on details that would otherwise escape the viewer's attention.
Extreme close-up shot	This is an extreme, superlative version of the close-up that shows, for example, only certain parts of the human face, such as the eyes and mouth, or details of an object, or perhaps objects that are important to the narrative. Details in the video have an emotional and suggestive impact.

The perspective of the camera always corresponds to the imaginary position of the viewer. What is fascinating about video is that, unlike in reality, you can change perspectives at lightning speed.

The perspective and viewing line of the camera, in conjunction with the shot size, forge the intrinsic relationship between the viewer and the object being depicted. This renders the camera capable of exaggeration and distortion.

Eye-level shot	The subject is shown at "eye level." Since the eye-level shot can appear static and monotonous, it is often replaced by a slightly high or low angle.
Extreme low-angle shot	The portrayed subject appears self-confident, superior, heroic, dominant; the viewer must look up to the protagonist.
Extreme high-angle/bird's-eye shot	Subjects shot from above give viewers the impression that they are hovering above everything filmed. The subject appears miserable, lonely, and small.

4.2 The Continuity of the Images

A video tells a story, but it tells it differently than a written text. It is conveyed to the viewer through a series of images. Every image embodies an idea, and every scene is a sequence of ideas. Together they form a harmonious progression. If this visual harmony and continuity is then violated, the viewer may become confused and lose the thread of the narrative.

The Direction of Movement

If, for example, a person appears in the frame from the left and leaves the frame on the right, he or she must come from the left again in the subsequent shot to resume the previously shown movement. If this were any different, the viewer would have to be informed as to why the direction of movement has changed. For instance, an intermediate cut could show how the person stops, looks as if he or she has forgotten something, and then turns around. This would explain the change in the direction of movement.

The Line of Action

Subject movements can confuse viewers if they are interrupted by a change of setting and the new camera position jumps over the line of action, which is the direction in which a process takes place. If the camera crosses this imaginary line of action, the viewer suddenly sees a reversal in the direction of the action. The left-right orientation in the image is lost, and the viewer becomes disoriented. A shot that "inadvertently reverses direction" by crossing this line is a classic mistake and violates the "180-degree rule". Hence, the camera should always remain on the same side of the line. The line of action can only be crossed and the direction reversed by a movement of the camera or by the protagonist(s). This can also be used to make a dialogue (a scene) more visually engaging and, for example, to mark or emphasize a turning point in the conversation.

Practical Tips for Shooting

Recording test	Before you actually start filming, make sure that the camera is recording correctly. Do a recording test for a few seconds, then play it back in the camera to check that it is working properly.
Natural lighting situations	Bright sources of light and windows should always be behind the camera when recording. Strong contrasts (bright background) are to be avoided by reducing the size of the frame, using the backlight button, or selecting the manual aperture control.
Frame	Moving objects should be filmed with a larger frame (medium long shot, possibly a full shot) to give the subject some space and to be able to react quickly enough should an unexpected change in direction occur. In the telephoto range, pay close attention to the focal plane. If the distance between the lens and the subject changes, the focus may need to be readjusted during recording. With telephoto settings (close-ups), the depth-of-field range is extremely small. Consequently, movements should be recorded with the widest possible angle.
Manual focus	Maximum zoom on the subject, focus, optimize the frame, and start recording! In most situations, it is worth working with manual focus. Almost all cameras have a button which, as long as it is depressed, activates the automatic focus. This can be used to adjust the focus if the time available or the circumstances do not allow you to focus the camera yourself. You have more control over the focus with the manual adjustment, though.
Camera movements	Slow panning! The viewer needs time to interpret the images. Simultaneous panning and zooming should be avoided; panning and zooming should have a specific purpose. The viewer expects to be shown something specific with a zoom or a pan (a clue of some sort). Aimlessly wandering camera shots, on the other hand, have a disorienting effect and can, at best, be used as a deliberate, stylistic method of expressing the restlessness of a protagonist.
Always keep the editing in mind	Two shots of the same subject should differ at least in terms of the shot size or the camera angle. If the difference in the image is not clear enough, the two shots will later appear to "jump" when edited together.
Scene lengths	Make sure that the recording is started well before the intended action and stopped again after the action is completed, even if it is a little too long, to avoid missing the recording of important information.

4.3 Conveying Knowledge with the Emotional Medium of Video

If you want to use video as a medium to convey knowledge and information, you should always keep in mind that images, with their symbolic meaning, appeal first and foremost to our emotions. Anyone who creates film scenes will always evoke an emotional response; and before you accidentally achieve the wrong one, you should make a deliberate effort to create intentional effects and steer the audience in a specific direction.

For example, if you jiggle your camera around, you are not drawing attention to the content of the images, but to the improperly operated equipment. Wobbly shots will make your viewers feel anxious and stressed. You should use a tripod whenever possible.

If scenes that are recognized in four seconds are left standing for twenty seconds, viewers will become bored. You should keep this rule of thumb in mind when shooting to avoid changing shots too quickly and too frequently, unless absolutely necessary.

At every shooting location, you need a clear concept for the images and sounds that are essential to the narrative. This applies both to staged and documentary work and to artistic-performative research. In any event, you have to think carefully about what you intend to tell viewers and which images you need for this narrative.

Should unexpected events influence the shooting, adaptations must be made without losing sight of the actual narrative. It is especially important to have internalized the overall concept in the event that unexpected situations arise. This allows you to react in a carefully considered manner to unanticipated developments at short notice.

Types of Cameras for Research Videos

Semiprofessional cameras	Semiprofessional cameras (for example, the Sony PXW-FS7) are relatively inexpensive, but still offer all the required functions to achieve excellent results. They have the necessary size to perform smooth camera movements and can be combined with professional auxiliary equipment. They tend to be too complex for absolute beginners, though. Semiprofessional cameras are best suited for recordings over a longer period of time because they are highly reliable and have a large storage capacity and long battery life.
Single-lens reflex (SLR) photo cameras with video recording capability	SLR cameras with video recording capability (such as the Canon 5F Mark 4) are very popular because they offer a combination of professionalism and handiness. Impressive moving images can be created quickly and easily. These cameras are very easy to transport. However, sound recording is limited and requires quite a few accessories for improved performance, which makes the camera slightly less handy to use.
Smartphones	Popular smartphone models (iPhone, Samsung Galaxy, etc.) have integrated high-resolution cameras that can compete with conventional camera models. Convenience, handiness, and speed are the main arguments here. Sound capabilities are limited here, too, and require accessories to achieve better quality. There are many innovative accessory solutions.
Action cams	Action cams are extremely small and very stable devices that can be mounted on helmets, handlebars, poles, and windshields. The shot is reduced to a single very wide angle setting so that the camera shoots as much as possible. These cameras are ideally suited to recordings of sporting or performative activities. They are waterproof and virtually indestructible. In terms of the scope of artistic creativity, however, you quickly reach your limits. Sound recording options are available but limited. No additional devices can be connected to the camera.
360-degree cameras	360-degree cameras are available from very small and handy types (such as the Ricoh 360) up to high-end models with outstanding recording quality (for example, the Insta360 Pro II). An image that allows you to turn your gaze 180 or 360 degrees offers many exciting possibilities and can be an ideal solution when observing a landscape or a room, for example. It is not possible to change the lens (wide angle to telephoto). Viewers can focus on different elements or angles in the same video, that is, they can experience the same video differently.

The phenomena and patterr
study are often only discove
research process. Video res
If they point the camera onl
the video may not produce
hand, they point the camera
raises the question of what
is new has not yet been rev
recording.

.hat are of relevance to the
d during the subsequent
chers thus face a paradox.
 what is already known,
 insights. If, on the other
 what is unknown, this
ould be filmed, since what
ed at the time of the

Editing Research:
Video Editing
Léa Klaue, Eric Andreae

The editing process gives meaning to moving images. It also extends far beyond the technical aspects of editing a film to encompass virtually the entire production process, from developing the initial idea for an image to selecting the right frame (framing), editing the material, adding soundtracks, making color corrections, creating subtitles, and cutting unwanted segments from the film. All decisions pertaining to the way the film narrative is conveyed are included in the editing process.

Videos are edited to make the filmed material more intelligible. During the editing process, decisions are made on the chronology of the narrative. For instance, what elements are presented to the audience first? The editing process renders the narrative more realistic and coherent. Video editing can intensify emotions, highlight specific aspects, and illustrate and convey complex narratives.

Video editing uses artistic interventions to transpose our three-dimensional reality to a two-dimensional medium. Editing can compress a story that unfolds over several days, weeks, or even years to an hour or less. Thus, the film does not depict "real time" but rather excerpts from different time intervals ("narrative time"). In academic, applied, and artistic research based on audio-visual tools, video editing varies depending on the goal of the research video. In the social sciences and fields of research that involve people or their activities, editing is an essential step that paves the way toward a deeper understanding of the material.

In an ethnographic film, as in a documentary film, scenes are structured much like in a feature film, with B-roll footage, voice-overs, and possibly music along with a variety of changing perspectives on the protagonists. Here the editing serves to reconstruct a sense of locality, people, and situations, while at the same time drawing attention to certain established facts or objects of research. For ethnographers, editing becomes a creative and subjective work in which they try to reconstruct a reality that only they (and a research team that may have been present) or the protagonists of the research have experienced in exactly the same way.

5.1 The Right Software for Video Editing

Software like Adobe Premiere Pro is generally used for video editing and provides functions that make it possible to import the associated video data via external hardware and compile it in a dedicated archive. If no external video sources are used, it is possible to integrate previously digitalized data into your project. You can add music to video data, insert still images, create transitions between clips, add sound effects, and include credits. Several video images can appear simultaneously, can be moved and manipulated, adjusted in terms of color and brightness, distorted, deformed, filtered, and blurred. Anyone who finds this too complicated can reduce any functionality to a few simple principles.

Generally speaking, video editing software requires a tidy, orderly working approach. A logical system of labeling embedded clips, sound files, still images, etc. is helpful, even for small projects: a short video can generate an archive with more than 150 elements. Files that are not being used should be removed from the project, and complex subsections should be cut into separate sequences. As is often the case with computer programs, video editing software offers a wide range of options that ultimately lead to the same goal. Everyone will develop their own method of working after a certain learning curve.

5.2   An Editing Process with a Plan and a Common Thread

Before you start editing, you should decide on the intention of your planned video. You may find it very helpful to outline a plan and—depending on the amount of video material—divide the video into chapters or subvideos. It is important that you have enough material to create the planned video and that you use the filmed material effectively. An initial review of all the material is helpful, and you should take notes and make lists.

If a great deal of material is available, it makes sense to create an overview document in which the material is listed chronologically and divided according to different locations, people, and/or topics. You can also note the type of images: interview, B-roll, event recording, sound recording, and so on. Such a document can be useful throughout the entire editing process when searching for specific images.

Filmmakers often underestimate how much time is needed for editing. Viewing alone requires considerable time, energy, and concentration. Allowing sufficient buffer time is an absolute must, especially if the production of the video is associated with a delivery deadline.

When planning the film, you should also think about what genre and what type of narrative format you intend to use. Popular forms include the classic journalistic short video and the "vlog" (video blog), which has a narrative character. In research and in the academic world in general, there are several styles that are often used. One of these is the observational film, in which the filmmakers attempt to make themselves as unobtrusive and discreet as possible to give viewers the impression that the film team was not even present at all: the "fly-on-the-wall" effect. Common terms for these types of documentary films include direct cinema, cinéma vérité, and observational cinema. In contrast to an observational film, as a filmmaker you may opt for other forms of narration to make your own authorship and presence on the film all the more apparent. One can work in a "journalistic" style by relying on a narrator (perhaps the filmmaker/researcher can also serve as the narrator) who is present on location and on camera, introduces the undertaking, adds commentary, and in doing so conveys their own perspective on the research.

A similar effect can be achieved with voice-over, in which the narrator tells the actual story and guides the viewer through the events. This can be written in a more personal first-person form, or it can endeavor to remain more factual, objective, and descriptive. The voice-over can also be used to highlight issues in the video that could not be filmed or that cannot be presented visually (such as a background story, abstract concepts, and statements by people who do not want to be filmed).

It is also good to incorporate an occasional "breather" into the video. Moments in which a large amount of information is presented–or information that is more "difficult to digest" and takes some time to be processed by the viewer–should be followed by brief breaks. These intermissions can include B-roll scenes, landscapes, or background images. Music can also be added, if appropriate. Such moments can also be used to integrate texts into the video. Inserting texts, subtitles, captions, or titles can help guide the viewer.

If you intend to present the video in connection with a text that is outside the medium of video, you must take this into account during the editing process. Where and in what context is the video presented? Will it be inserted in the middle of a text on a website or next to an information panel in an exhibition? A voice-over that repeats exactly the same message as a text that the audience has already read before watching the video is counterproductive and tiresome.

The editing process should have a common thread. It is only when you have established the concept of the video and know exactly what story you intend to present, and in what form, that you can begin editing by selecting those parts of the video material that tell that story. These elements are placed on the timeline of the editing program. When all of the pieces that you want to include on the timeline are in the desired order, you have completed the rough cut. You can polish the rough cut and make modifications until you have created the intended statement and storyline.

From the rough cut, you proceed to the fine cut phase, in which you polish minor details: more precise beginnings and endings of sequences, sound corrections, insertion of B-roll material, etc. Fine-cutting also involves adjusting the rhythm of the entire video by closely examining the interplay of images and statements. Are only "talking heads" visible throughout the video? Or do you only see landscapes? A deliberate interplay of different settings renders the video more rhythmic and engaging, while an endless string of similar settings and repetitive statements can be quite tedious.

If necessary, colors can be corrected after the fine cut. At this point, you can add music, sound effects, or extra sounds as well as titles, lyrics, subtitles, and the credits.

It is important that the finished video be viewed as often as possible and shown to different people to obtain feedback. This provides an opportunity to correct any problems—elements that are poorly understood or even misunderstood—before the project is completed.

The best way to judge whether the editing has rendered the narrative coherent is to watch the video once again at a later date, after you have gained some distance from it. During the editing process, it is essential to allow for time in which you are not working on the editing, so you can look at the video again with fresh eyes and make any necessary adjustments.

5.3 Annotating

The Research Video annotation tool can be applied to any type of video, whether or not it was produced specifically for annotation. When working with the annotation tool, it is helpful to divide the video into several segments. Annotations draw attention to particular aspects of the video and highlight their importance, so it makes sense to create chapters and divide the video according to various topics. It is easier to take stock of several short videos, each with a dozen annotations, than of a single, long video with a very large number of annotations.

If you present a video with annotations, shorter and more straightforward videos are more viewer-friendly. The mp4 with H.264 Codec format is recommended for smooth importing and exporting with the Research Video annotation tool.

5.4 Image Sequences and Editing Styles

Sequences of images merge into a single, cohesive entity in the viewer's perception, even if they are spatially and temporally separated. One image can have an inductive influence on the meaning and interpretation of the next one, and missing images are imagined in the mind of the viewer. The following approaches illustrate the principles behind the editing process.

Editing Styles

Narrative cuts	Space and time are structured and interrelated, jumps in time can be concealed. Films and videos rarely portray a series of events in real time; instead, they are condensed with omissions and jumps in time. (An individual packs a backpack. Cut. In the next scene, that same person is walking toward a hill. Cut. The person reaches the top.) The intervening details–how the person exits the house, etc.–are omitted, since the viewers are capable of piecing together these missing bits in their own minds.
Causal cuts	Shots that show a cause can be linked to shots that show an effect. If children are playing a ball game and a child kicks a particularly hard shot , then a cut to either the shattering glass (an off-camera sound effect, the window cannot be seen) or a visibly bursting window pane would be associated with the child's action in the previous separate sequence.
Parallel cuts	Two spatially separate, but related actions are alternately intercut, switching the narrative back and forth between the two. This is a common dramaturgical means of creating suspense.
Rhythmic cuts	Short shots can create the illusion of fast motion; long shots can convey an impression of calm. Everyone unconsciously notices when an image remains on screen for too long. This, in turn, creates a sense of unease. The duration of the action depends on the image size, the storyline, and the desired effect.
Contrast cutting	When, for example, pictures of beggars and slums are combined with glamorous images of high society, a contrast is created. Striking image contrasts are easily perceived as symbols of real contrasts (in the example: poverty vs. wealth).

Léa Klaue, Eric Andreae

Audio Track

Language	Language can be introduced as commentary, a monologue, or a dialogue.
Sounds	Sounds can accentuate actions.
Music	Music can amplify or induce moods or connect scenes.
Silence	Silence can create contrasts or amplify the sounds that precede or follow it.

6

Analyzing Videos:
Selecting an Approach and Annotating
Gunter Lösel

In the field of artistic research, there is such a wide array of research traditions to choose from that no single approach can be assumed a priori as the most appropriate one. At the outset of a research project using video and annotations, how can researchers find their bearings within the landscape of investigative methodologies without constraining themselves to a strictly defined approach? This chapter illustrates different ways of flagging, arranging, organizing, analyzing, and annotating relevant segments, even when dealing with large amounts of video material.

Analyzing videos is an undertaking that is never entirely free of preconceived notions, and the first step for researchers is to find their bearings within the field of possible research approaches and thus reflect on their own basic assumptions. In 2018 René Tuma presented an overview of the leading research traditions that are of importance within the context of video analysis.

This classification (→ fig. 01) illustrates the historical evolution of these approaches; that is, it examines how they are embedded in existing theories. In keeping with the objectives of our project, we have sought to overcome these disciplinary constraints.

6.1 Setting the Course for Your Own Project

Is my research about manifest or latent patterns? The approaches can be classified according to whether they tend to focus on the surface or the deep structure of the data. Gubrium and Holstein describe this as the interaction between the "whats"–the concrete, describable content–and the "hows"–the contexts that are not directly observable and hence need to be explored (Gubrium and Holstein 1997). Accordingly, the different approaches can also be classified according to whether they primarily examine the "what" or the "how" of the material.

This decision (→ fig. 02) determines, among other things, which and how much data is to be collected. Whereas the search for manifest patterns usually requires a broad database, the focus on latent patterns is usually confined to small yet well-selected sets of data. So, by deciding between "manifest and latent", you also determine the extent to which your research is broad (breadth) or narrow (depth).

For instance, artistic research often investigates processes that are not conscious and declarative. Instead, it is "tacit knowledge" that must first be rendered observable and describable through specific approaches. Artistic research, therefore, often addresses latent structures (however, unlike other hermeneutic methods, this does not involve the reconstruction of latent structures of meaning, but rather a wealth of intuitive, corporeal, material-related, and other approaches that "somehow" lead to an artistically relevant output). The associated research aims to reveal these invisible structures and incorporated practices. In other instances, though, artistic research also deals with the explicit, declarative knowledge of the artists, which can be explored

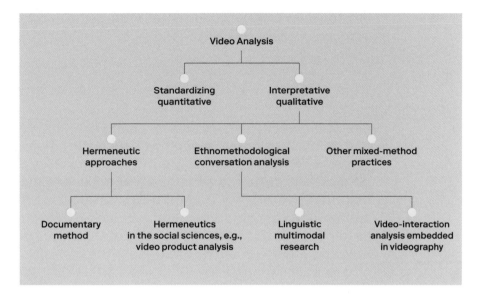

01

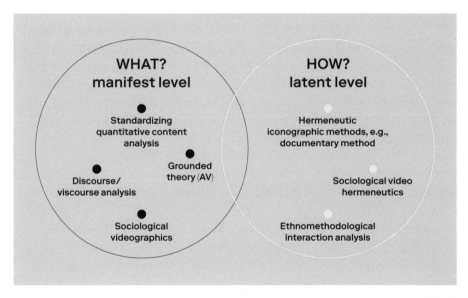

02

Fig. 01:
Video analysis method proposed by
René Tuma (Source: Tuma 2018, p. 426)

Fig. 02:
"What" and "How" of the analysis
(illustration by author)

in interviews or video-cued recall situations. In such circumstances, it seeks manifest content or "declarative knowledge".

What Elements of the Video Material Should Be Examined?

A radical response would be: everything that has been recorded and as much as possible should be recorded. This is the approach taken by the visual grounded theory (Mey and Dietrich 2016). The documentary method also applies to the recorded material in its entirety (Burkhard 2018). Here it is a matter of sifting through vast amounts of data because the sought-after patterns (such as the individual style of the author) are not found here and there, but rather throughout the material.

As a rule, though, a selection is made, that is, only selected key sequences are examined. This applies to all hermeneutic methods. Selecting these segments, commonly known as sampling, thus becomes a critical process, which must be well justified from a methodological standpoint.

In extreme cases, only tiny fragments of the video are used (perhaps only individual stills). This applies, for example, to methods derived from image analysis, such as figurative hermeneutics (Eisewicht et al. 2018), in which it is perfectly feasible to work with individual images. But even objective hermeneutics, as envisioned by Ulrich Oevermann, can make do with very little data (Oevermann et al. 1979).

What Context Should I Use for Interpretation?

Researchers can approach an issue or a phenomenon with an abundance of previous knowledge or they can attempt to comprehend it on their own accord. Different research approaches can come into play here:

No context. The manifestation is examined under the premise of being devoid of any context (such as in objective hermeneutics). This makes it possible to approach the sample without bias, and it leads to unconventional interpretations. Consequently, the context has to be "hidden," as if only one part of an image were examined by covering the rest with paper.

Only context that is accessible to the respective players in the field at a specific time. The goal here is to reconstruct this knowledge from the perspective of the players, not from the bird's-eye view of the researchers. Accordingly, it is not permitted to use information presented later in the video to interpret earlier states, as this information exceeds the knowledge of the players at the given time. Such an approach corresponds, for instance, to the basic assumptions of ethnomethodology.

All case-specific information, that is, the contexts created by the video itself. For example, phenomena in the video can be explained by information that appears later in the material.

All case-specific information plus any details that are directly related to the creation of the video, such as news announcements, interviews, production materials like screenplays, etc. The context is extended here to allow for a multiperspective analysis.

The entire world knowledge of the researcher (for example, figural hermeneutics, grounded theory).

The entire world knowledge of the individual researcher plus the world knowledge of a group of researchers.
Videography, for example, relies on this approach (Tuma 2018).

The researcher(s) should select the interpretive framework that corresponds to the respective goals of the concrete project.

How Is the Action Behind the Camera Analyzed?

Depending on the approach used, different types of video constitute the basis of the analysis. Videos that are found online or that become available in another form as finished products raise completely different questions than those that are created under the watchful eye of a researcher specifically for the purpose of conducting a study. With previously existing videos, in addition to the content, or the on-camera action, the action behind the camera constitutes a focal point of the analysis because it goes beyond the physical recording of images and encompasses the entire range of postproduction steps, including all decisions on camera angles, framing, light, depth of field, editing, effects, etc.

It is always necessary to establish to what extent the action behind the camera is part of the analysis, and hence to identify, transcribe, and analyze its elements accordingly. With videos produced specifically for research purposes, the action behind the camera reflects the intention of generating knowledge and is thus an integral part of the method. It must be assessed to determine its suitability for achieving the goal of the research and rendered transparent. Depending on the research objective, one or the other aspect can be given more weight, but both levels should always be included in the analysis (Reichertz 2018).

How Important Is Selective and Subjective Perception?

In striving to achieve the ideal of an "objective camera", researchers aim to minimize the degree to which they preselect material and seek to capture a wide range of information, maintaining a broad "data focus". Ideally, the camera endeavors to capture "simply everything", which of course can never be entirely achieved.

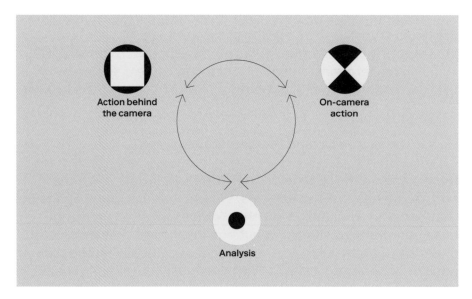

03

Fig. 03:
Action behind the camera as part of
the analysis (illustration by author)

By erecting a 360-degree camera, researchers admittedly come closer to this ideal than was previously possible, but here, too, preliminary decisions are made, for example, on where to place the camera. Instead of an "objective camera", the work proceeds with a "subjective camera", which requires that clear decisions be made at the time of shooting, decisions that, out of artistic and analytical considerations, often have to be made very quickly and intuitively. The video data is then, of course, highly selective. Since the assumption of objectivity is subsequently no longer tenable, the active, subjective action behind the camera must be included as part of the analysis. We can conceptualize the different types of audiovisual data as a continuum:

$$\text{Subjective} \longleftrightarrow \text{Objective}$$

Varying degrees of subjectivity require different methods of analysis. Researchers need to make such decisions "before they start filming".

Top-Down or Bottom-Up?

All research approaches are based on a common understanding that new knowledge is always engendered by the interaction of theoretical concepts and newly acquired data. But there are differences in the sequencing and weighting: What comes first? What is more important?

Although the concepts may vary, a distinction can be made between top-down approaches, which derive practical applications from theoretical concepts that are then tested against the data, and bottom-up approaches, which examine the data with a minimum of preconceived notions in a bid to identify emerging patterns. Most methods alternate between bottom-up and top-down phases (older, related terms for these phases are inductive and deductive).

Top-down approach (→ fig. 04): The theoretical concept, here displayed as a yellow circle with black spot, is used to establish categories that can then be used to detect the corresponding phenomena in the data or, if the phenomena cannot be found, to call into question the concept.

Bottom-up approach (→ fig. 05): The data (observations) come first and constitute the outset. By applying epistemic practices, patterns become recognizable; they "emerge," or rise to the surface, and are only then theoretically categorized and put into words.

6.2 Analyzing with Videos and Annotations

Once the researchers' own position and methods have been clarified, the data is collected, processed accordingly, and subsequently presented in a form that fits the respective research design. Annotations can be added as live annotations when the video data is recorded (for example, with the Piecemaker2Go tool) and, in any number of steps of analysis, can later be supplemented with more annotations, resulting in what anthropologist Clifford Geertz calls a "thick description" (Geertz 2017). According to our model in the introduction, this corresponds to "enriched data."

Already when formulating annotations, preliminary findings will emerge, which in turn are noted down and provide the material for further steps of analysis. In this respect, the transition from data collection to data analysis is often seamless. In the following sections, we will describe the individual stages as distinct from one another, which, in reality, is rarely the case.

Description of the Data

The first step of data analysis is always a summary description of the data. What types of data are actually available? What is their scope and quality? Quantitative approaches rely on "descriptive statistics" for this purpose, whereas qualitative approaches involve laying out the complete data material and compiling a textual description of the data types, for example, as a table, field notes, or a logbook. The diverse video data is labeled and subjected to an initial review.

Jürgen Raab and Marija Stanisavljevic recommend sifting through all the material first without taking notes. They say that it is only after this overall impression has been achieved that notes should be taken during a second review (Raab and Stanisavljevic 2018). Other methods recommend a logbook or a rough classification in the form of a list or a table. When working with videos, a good filing system for video files and a good file identification system is absolutely essential for screening the material. Descriptions should also include a critical evaluation of the data.

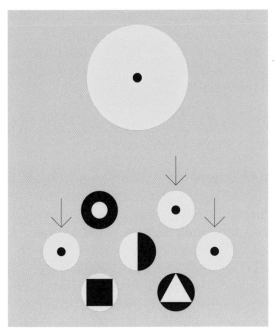

04

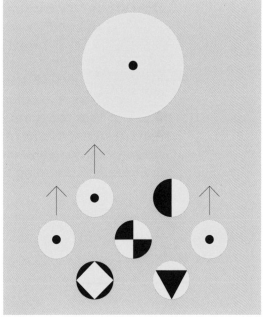

05

Fig. 04:
Top-down approach
(illustration by author)

Fig. 05:
Bottom-up approach
(illustration by author)

Creating an overview also compels you to complete the data collection phase at some point. A research project is not an endless journey, but rather a process that moves toward an end, which is why it is important to complete the transition from one phase before proceeding to the next one.

Defining the Unit of Analysis

What is the smallest unit to be examined, that is, the "unit of analysis"? It is usually possible to derive the answer from the theory and the context of the study. How big are the phenomena under study? If we intend to catch small fish, we need a close-meshed net, but if we are looking to catch big fish, we use a wide-meshed net. And if we don't know what kind of fish we want to catch, we should take samples and decide afterward. For instance, microsociological studies require completely different units of analysis than sociological discourse analyses. Ramey et al. (2016) point out that the units of analysis can change during the research process and argue in favor of a flexible, iterative approach. When conducting video analyses, the unit of investigation can vary greatly depending on the design of the research.

Unit of Investigation for Video Analyses

Very fine	The smallest analyzable units are stills of the video, that is, single images or frames. This is the unit of choice for image-interpreting procedures such as figurative hermeneutics, which are derived from the analysis of still images.
Fine	The units of analysis here are moves, that is, the smallest of meaningful movements. Moves are roughly comparable to words: you can interpret them individually, because each word carries a meaning, but they are all merely elements of an interaction. One example might be a gesture made during an utterance, or an emotional expression that accompanies one. Such phenomena can also occur subliminally in the range of microseconds. In such instances, they only become apparent when watching the video in slow-motion mode.
Middle	Here the unit of analysis is a single interaction element or turn, in which the participants themselves mark the beginning and end of a turn with metapragmatic signals (Goffman 1974). The analysis avoids an "artificial" segmentation and instead follows the "natural" course of events (interaction analysis and conversation analysis).
At the scale of the individual	Here, the focus is on the individual components of action that reflect the strategy, style, or habitus of the respective participant in the interaction. The units of analysis here do not relate to a particular interaction, but rather to a specific individual, and hence they are scattered throughout the material wherever an expression appears "typical" of that person. Such units can be described in terms of their intentionality or functionality, for example, an interaction where A aims to instruct B in a certain way, which can be brought to light in the analysis. A similar idea is the "habitus" concept proposed by Pierre Bourdieu.
Societal	This pertains to social systems and discourses and comprise sequences of communications and actions in the public sphere that make reference to one another but do not necessarily constitute part of the immediate interaction, for example, diverse critiques of a theater production at different times and in different places. The units of analysis in such discourse and viscourse analyses can be of any size and may comprise huge amounts of data.

By displaying the size of the annotation on the track in Research Video, the software provides a direct visualization of the unit of analysis. This makes the tool well suited for determining units of analysis. They are reflected in the size of the annotations on the tracks. In a use case, for example, the acts and scenes of a feature film were dissected using annotations (→ fig. 6).

How Do I Find Relevant Passages in the Material (Sampling)?

After the data has been described, it is usually necessary to identify smaller sequences that are relevant to the analysis. This process, known as sampling, becomes increasingly important as more and more material is selected. There are several recognized methods.

Methods of Sampling

Theoretical sampling	The selection is closely related to the research thesis, and the researcher only selects sequences that are related to the thesis based on theoretical considerations.
Whole-to-part method	Multiple viewers look at the entire data corpus and endeavor to reach a consensus on the relevant passages (Erickson 2006).
Representative sampling	With this option, a "typical" sample is selected from a collection of similar data. The selection is validated intersubjectively by consulting experts.
Selection based on "narrative power"	Derry et al. regard this form of selection as legitimate, in which clips are selected that support the narrative of the research. The story is told with a "disciplined subjectivity" that does not claim to reflect objective perspectives, but is not purely fictional either.
Iterative sampling	Derry et al. do not see sampling as a self-contained step. Instead, they understand it as an iterative process that occurs repeatedly throughout the course of the research, so that one sampling can lead to another sampling.

Raab and Stanisavljevic (2018) propose the following procedure:

○ View all material, without taking notes
○ Second review with notes
○ Select a passage that could be relevant to the research question
○ Conduct a detailed analysis of the key segment
○ Select additional segments that display minimum contrast
○ Select additional segments that display maximum contrast

This method for the formation of minimum/maximum contrasts is described in greater detail in chapter 8.

Indeed, sampling is one of the key practices of qualitative research, even if the selection is by no means as methodologically precise as is occasionally claimed. In the widespread "snowball system," for example, segments are identified simply by the fact that several viewers agree that they are "somehow interesting." Consequently, selecting the relevant sequences remains to a certain extent subjective and intuitive, no matter how methodically the researchers have worked.

Research Video offers excellent options to split a video into sequences and visualize them. By having the same material sampled by different researchers, a certain intersubjective validation can be quickly and clearly achieved. This makes the tool a sound basis for sampling, regardless of which method is used.

Transcription

The process of analyzing the data also entails transcription as a means of describing observable phenomena. All research approaches include transcription as a necessity element, and it has been pointed out many times that all transcriptions contain preliminary decisions that significantly influence the subsequent course of the research: "To create a transcript is to make consequential choices about which phenomena merit representation" (Ramey 2016, p. 2).

The transcription thus generates a "conceptual lens", or selective perception, which must be well thought out and justified because it determines what the researchers perceive in the first place and what they might overlook. In addition to language, a wide range of modalities of conduct have been transcribed into videos: gestures, glances, body postures, facial expressions, movement, material objects, etc.

Each research tradition and research thesis determines how fine and how multimodal a transcription should be, for example, whether it should include unconscious or subliminal behavior like throat clearing, pauses, swallowing, hesitation sounds, etc. The transcription also determines how the action behind the camera is to be incorporated into the research.

There are systems and tools for transcription in the respective research traditions, which can be classified as follows (Moritz in Moritz and Corsten 2018, p. 14): "Tools like HIAT, ELAN, and EX-MARaLDA are suitable for research that focuses more on spoken language. Field Score, MoviScript, and TraVis are all suitable tools for social scientific analysis. Other software such as Akira, AT-LAS.ti, MAXQDA and NVivo bypass transcription entirely and deal with specific methods of evaluation, for instance, within the context of qualitative content analysis." An overview of the different available tools is provided by Moritz (2014).

Annotated video software like Research Video offers outstanding transcription options in which the respective tracks can be freely filled with content as desired. Both linguistic and non-verbal cues can be entered, in addition to aspects of the action behind the camera. Researchers can also expand these transcription modalities during the analysis.

Data Analysis: Pattern Recognition

Knowledge manifests itself in patterns and contexts. The epistemic (cognition-enabling) function of a video becomes clear when it presents opportunities to see data in a new way, to rearrange it, filter it differently, and recognize patterns that would otherwise remain hidden to the naked eye. The analysis begins with concrete perception and gradually progresses to more complex processing, just as the eye processes perceptual data first, followed by the visual cortex and then other parts of the brain. In artistic research, this is not so much a process of verification or falsification, but rather one of perceptual amplification.

The recognized patterns do not necessarily have to be causal patterns–although these are preferred in experimental research–but may just as well consist of phenomenological patterns, that is, those that allow us to perceive a context differently. You can imagine it as analogous to the edge detection ability of a computer, which allows it to clearly distinguish different surfaces by emphasizing transitions. The computer compares points of perception with their immediate surroundings and calculates the degree of similarity. This method enables machines to perceive contours and recognize objects. The human brain has a similar mechanism that enhances contrasts where an area ends, so that objects stand out sharply from the background (shape perception).

Similarly, the analysis of video material using the formation of minimum/maximum contrasts can precisely pinpoint such differences and trace their exact progression. This process can also be compared to the use of contrasting agents in biological and medical research. Based on certain practices, the data is "colored" in such a way that patterns are rendered visible (→ fig. 7).

By using tracks as observation categories, such patterns can be immediately made visible in Research Video. If you hide individual tracks, these patterns become even more visible. This not only makes them more vivid, but also makes them comprehensible to other researchers who would like to retrace the process from screening the original video material to drawing the final conclusions. Consequently, the interpretation remains closely bound with the material and can be called into question by other viewers. Do they see the same phenomenon as the researchers? The analysis thus remains available to be challenged and intersubjectively validated.

Recommended Reading

Derry et al. (2010) have developed a comprehensive set of guidelines. They focus on four problems: selection, analysis, technology, and ethics. Another useful source is the paper by Ramey et al. (2016) for a symposium on standards and heuristics of video analysis, which formulates the rules of thumb for tackling key problems.

06

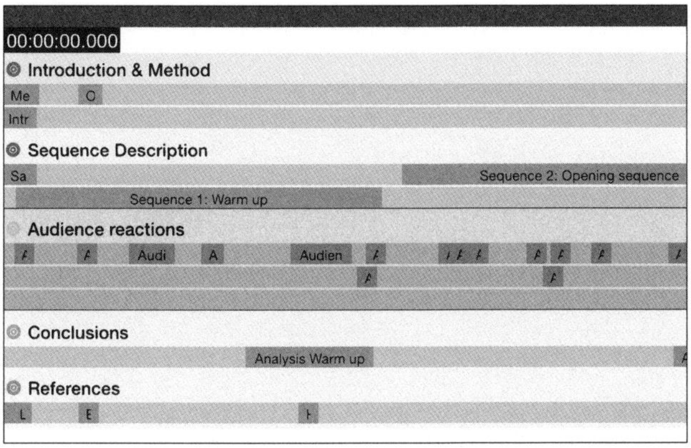

07

Fig. 06:
Sequencing with tracks and annotations

Fig. 07:
Sample project: annotations illustrate the rhythm of the audience's reactions.

The recognized patterns do causal patterns—although experimental research—but phenomenological patterns us to perceive a context dif

necessarily have to be
se are preferred in
ay just as well consist of
at is, those that allow
ently.

Publishing a Research Video:
Uploading to the Media Archive
Martin Grödl, Moritz Resl

This guide will show you how to publish your Research Video project on the ZHdK Media Archive.

Please note: This guide contains some basic actions that are dependent on your operating system, such as renaming files, extracting archives, and editing text files. The guide is written from the perspective of a macOS user. Please adapt accordingly if you are using a different OS.

Before you can start you have to get your personal login by sending an e-mail to research.video@zhdk.ch. Please specify:

○ Name of the project
○ First and last name
○ E-mail address
○ Date of expiration of required access

You will receive an e-mail as soon as your login has been created.

Step-by-Step Guide

Step 1	Export your RV Project

01 In Research Video, select the Project button.
02 Select Export in the Project pop-up.
03 Select OK when you are asked if you want to export an archive of your project.

Step 2	Rename downloaded file from .rv to .zip

01 Right-click the downloaded .rv file and select Rename.
02 Change the file extension from .rv to .zip. If prompted, confirm that you want to change the file's extension.

Are you sure you want to change the extension from ".rv" to ".zip"?

If you make this change, your document may open in a different application.

Keep .rv   Use .zip

Step 3

Extract ZIP file

This will give you two files:

○ video.m4v, which is the video file used in your project;
○ project.json, which contains all the annotations you made in Research Video.

Both of these files will be uploaded to the Media Archive in the following steps.

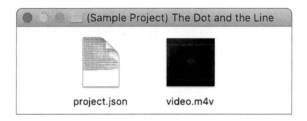

Step 4

Upload video to Media Archive

01 Log in to the Media Archive at https://medienarchiv.zhdk.ch.
02 Select Upload Media.
03 Upload video.m4v from the previous step and wait until the upload is finished.
04 Select Complete media entries.

Step 5   Add required information

01 Select the incomplete media entry video.m4v.
02 Select the Edit metadata button, the small pencil icon on the top right
    corner.

03 Add the required information:
    ○ a meaningful title
    ○ the copyright holder

04 Select Alle Daten and then RESEARCH VIDEO.
05 Paste the contents of the project.json file that you extracted previously
    into the box Research Video annotations:
    ○ Right-click the project.json file to open it.
    ○ Select Edit → Select All, then select Edit → Copy to copy all the .json
       data.
    ○ Back in the Media Archive, select the Research Video annotations box,
       then right-click and select Paste. The .json data should appear in the
       box.
06 Save the changes.

Step 6   Set permissions (optional)

This step is necessary if you want to share your Research Video project
with people outside of the Media Archive.

01 On the Media entry page, select Permissions.
02 Select Edit.

03 Select the View checkbox in the row Public/Internet.
04 In the same row, select the checkbox Download original & browse PDF.
05 Save the changes.

Step 7

Get a shareable URL

Your upload is now complete, but you still need to generate a unique URL so you can view and share your Research Video.

01 First copy the URL of your Media Archive entry.
02 Go to https://rv.zhdk.ch/madek-link, paste your URL and select <u>Get RV link</u>.
03 A Research Video URL will be generated. Select the <u>Copy</u> button or copy it manually.
04 This is the link to your Research Video published on the ZHDK Media Archive! If you set the permissions in Step 6, anybody with this link can view your published Research Video.

Step 8

Add URL to Media Archive entry (optional)

It is good practice to store the Research Video URL with the associated Media Archive entry.

01 Back at https://medienarchiv.zhdk.ch select the <u>Edit</u> button in your Media entry.
02 Select <u>Objekt</u> and scroll down to <u>Internet Links</u> (URL).

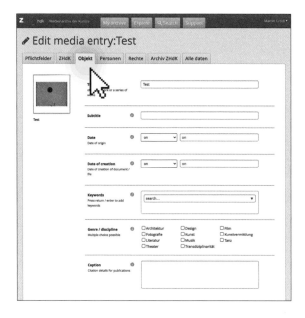

03 Enter a link identifier such as "Research Video Link:" and paste the URL.

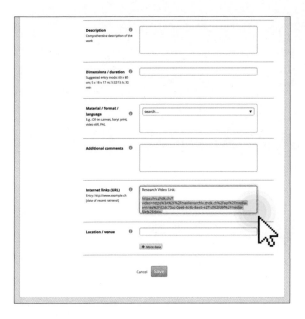

04 Save the changes.

The URL will now appear on your Media entry page and links directly to the Research Video application.

This process will take up to one hour. After that the researcher can share his or her Research Video project by simply sending the URL.

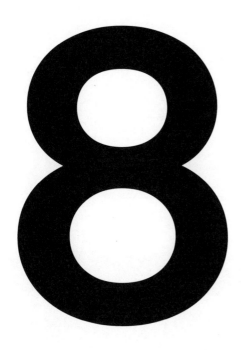

Publishing Research:
Academic Conventions, Videos, and Annotations
Gunter Lösel

Unlike text-based publications such as monographs, book sections, and articles, the new medium of annotated video has neither a long tradition in the academic world nor specific scholarly structures. The necessary conventions still need to be developed. This chapter focuses on the publication of "video articles" containing the findings of a specific research project.

8.1 Minimum Requirements

Many of the demands placed on scholarly work, such as the traditional quality criteria of validity and reliability, depend on individual research traditions. Because these criteria are discussed differently in each discipline, we will limit ourselves to two more general ones:

○ Shareability
The publication must be available to the research community (and, according to current requirements for open access publications, this availability cannot be subject to a fee or blocked by other access barriers).

○ Challengeability
Other researchers must be able to critically evaluate the publication. In other words, the methodology and exact process of knowledge generation must be transparent so that other researchers can understand and verify them.

8.2 Shareability of the Research Video

To meet the criterion of shareability, a publication must be <u>transportable</u> and <u>unchangeable</u>. A book meets these conditions in an exemplary way: it can be sent all over the world and will always have the same content for decades or even centuries; the same content in the same, precisely definable place.

This is not a given for digital objects but requires a technical solution. Digital objects are easily transportable, but are highly unstable and susceptible to change.

Creating a Permanent Link

For a Research Video project to be permanently locatable, it must be uploaded to a repository or a journal and assigned a permanent object identifier (such as a DOI number). From that point on, modification must be impossible–the file must be technically "frozen" and protected from subsequent change. We have defined a workflow in which a research video can be uploaded to the repository of the Zurich University of the Arts, where it is assigned a permanent link (→ see Chap. 7). The next step is to combine this link with the Research Video tool, which in turn generates a (very long) link. This final link, which can be transmitted and distributed, opens the research video in view-only mode.

View-Only Mode

In view-only mode, most functions are disabled. Although the viewer/reader sees the same interface used by authors, he or she cannot add or delete annotations, tracks, or tags. Nevertheless, the interface has a number of interactive features: the viewer/reader can move the playback bar, display annotations in the Inspector, hide tracks, and select tags from a drop-down menu. This process ensures the shareability of Research Video projects.

8.3 Challengeability

Citability

We propose using conventions from film studies. When scholars in this field cite a specific scene in a film, they use the following citation formula:

(Director, Production year, Timecode)

There are different styles as to how to cite the timecode, here is one example:

(Christopher Nolan, 2005, TC: 00:14:03–00:15:52)

The start and end of the sequence are given. If reference is made to just one frame, a single timecode is all that is needed. Citations of annotated videos can follow the same logic. If an annotation is cited, the start is given with just a single timecode. In order to make clear that it is an annotation, we suggest adding an "a" (lowercase) to the citation formula. An annotation in a Research Video project would thus be cited like this:

Director, Year of production, a-time code

(Christopher Nolan, 2005, a-TC: 00:14:03)

This is a very precise way to cite an annotation. In the highly unlikely event that several annotations start the same second, they can be numbered, just as publications are numbered when an author publishes several during a single year.

⟨Christopher Nolan, 2005, a-TC: 00:14:03[1]⟩
⟨Christopher Nolan, 2005, a-TC: 00:14:03[2]⟩
etc.

Methodological Transparency

For a publication to be challengeable, its authors must include detailed information about the research method used. A Research Video project is ideally suited for this, as it usually presents the data analysis process in a transparent way and shows parts of the research material. The reader is given a direct understanding of the categories that have been defined and how these categories relate to the specific research material.

However, researchers must also share the context of their research–that is, the theories they have drawn on as well as the concepts, terminology, and research methods employed. They typically provide information about the precise data collection process and the steps of data acquisition. Finally, they discuss their conclusions and the implications for their research field. It is not easy to embed such information in a video, and the question of how this can be done was one of the more difficult ones we faced in our project. Here are our proposed solutions, neither of which is perfect:

Researchers as "talking heads": A simple solution would be to film the researcher while he or she presents the above information. The corresponding clips could then be incorporated into the research video and annotated with more in-depth references. This is easy from a technical perspective, but requires researchers who are willing to appear before the camera.

Graphic visualization: This solution entails visualizing the information and recording it in the video. Options range from the simple filming of charts to complex animations, depending on the technical possibilities. As in ⟨1⟩, these clips could then be incorporated into the video and annotated with more in-depth information. Here we recommend working with trained designers from fields such as "motion design", "visual communication", and "knowledge visualization".

8.4 The Structure of a Research Publication

In addition to these minimum requirements, there are established structures for the presentation of research articles, such as the relatively simple, widely used IMRaD model.

IMRaD model

○ Introduction
○ Methods
○ Results
○ and Discussion

When it comes to applying this model to video publications, it is worth noting that the model is based on a temporal structure and thus tells a story. The Introduction describes the current state of research before the start of the research project and identifies a gap in research, a question or a problem. In the Methods section, the author provides a detailed description of the steps taken to generate new knowledge. This section usually covers all processes, from data collection to data analysis. In other words, it recounts all the actions taken to fill the gap in research and answer the research question. In the following Results section, the author presents the research findings. In the final Discussion section, the author re-embeds the new knowledge in the research context, discusses alternative interpretations of the findings, and formulates new research needs as a starting point for subsequent researchers.

Our question was: could we transfer the IMRaD structure to an annotated video? Today, our answer is: not on a one-to-one basis. The IMRaD structure was not conducive to the presentation of research material in any of our use cases. It proved to be difficult to structure the information such that the reader could see the "introduction" first, then the "method", and so on. Instead, videos make it possible to provide the information in parallel tracks. On a superficial level, though, researchers can at least imitate the IMRaD model: in several use cases, our researchers created tracks for "methods", "observations", "analysis", and "discussion" that built on the IMRaD model but did not represent a chronology (→ fig. 01).

Instead of understanding structure as a series of successive sections of an article, readers can see and process it as parallel tracks. They can view the different sections of the video in their

own chosen order, which enhances the sections' interactivity and comprehensibility.

The IMRaD model, seen through the lens of the research video, seems very artificial and one-dimensional. Even when it was possible to transfer the model to an annotated video, the chronology of the IMRaD structure was never really supported by the multitemporal logic of the research video. This came as a surprise and can be seen as evidence that textual forms of publication create a perceptual framework that is incompatible with the multiperspective, multitemporal framework established in the context of an annotated video. However, further studies are needed to validate this conclusion.

Structure as a Process of "Coloring" Data

The fact that a research paper reconstructs the temporal structure of the research process is certainly important for the publication of a video as a temporal medium. We therefore propose presenting the story of the research process chronologically, though not artificially segmented as in the IMRaD model. Instead, we suggest basing the story of the research process on the actual movements of the researchers (→ for more, see Chap. 9). During the video analysis phase, for example, researchers switch between a detailed analysis of the material and the theoretical level of concepts and terminology.

This process resembles the forward-and-backward movements of a painter who repeatedly steps away from the canvas and then moves back toward it. Researchers make an analogous movement: they step very close to the subject, study details, merge with the phenomenon, then distance themselves again to gain a more detached view. In other words, they switch back and forth between macro- and microanalysis in the generation of new knowledge (→ fig. 02).

The analysis usually starts at the macro level, with researchers gaining an overview of the material in its entirety. The next step is to divide the material into appropriate sections based on the chosen method and questions. Proceeding from this rough coding, researchers identify key sequences (samplings) on the basis of the research question and/or the underlying theoretical assumptions (Glaser and Strauss 2010).

It is important to identify an initial key sequence (S 1), as it is here that the detailed analysis begins. The detailed analysis then attempts, using one strategy or another, to cause the research-ers' suppositions to germinate, allowing new perceptions and interpretations. This is usually achieved by moving very close to the material and remaining in front of it for a longer time. The de-tailed analysis may be protracted and involve several persons and phases. It is deemed "complete" when the interpretive space becomes saturated, that is, when no new interpretations arise.

At some point, a new supposition will emerge. We call this the "structural hypothesis" (SH) because it condenses and re-structures the material. This structural hypothesis forms the basis of a new round of reflections at the macro level. In other words, at the theoretical and conceptual level, researchers look for new connections that incorporate or differentiate the structural hypothesis. Based on these reflections, they then seek sequences of the material that can support and expand the newly formed structural hypothesis. This process is called "minimum contrast formation".

If such a sequence (S 2) is found, it is once again subjected to detailed analysis, which leads to a new structural hypothesis. The second structural hypothesis (SH 2) may be identical to the first or elaborate on it and thus lead to further reflections at the macro level. The researcher can now comb through the material for sequences that are as dissimilar as possible to the identified phenomenon and may even contradict the structural hypothesis. This process is called "maximum contrast formation". This pro-duces a heightened awareness of contrasts; similarities and dif-ferences become more prominent.

This process is not so much about verification or falsification but about strengthening perception, and it can be narrated as such. A research video makes this mode of presentation possible. Video sequences that present theoretical reflections can be followed by sequences showing detailed analyses, allowing the viewer to understand the process by which data are "colored" and by which patterns gradually become visible.

In this chapter, we have suggested which academic conven-tions should be transferred to the research video as a new publi-cation format and how this can be achieved. The process is associated with many uncertainties, which we approached heu-ristically in our project. Using the analogy of established text-based formats, we investigated related standards, working on the premise that we should remain as independent as possible from disciplinary conventions and define only minimal requirements.

Finally, the potential of a productive, alternative, epistemic perspective should not be sacrificed in the effort to comply with existing conventions. After all, the goal is to further develop and give greater visibility to the specific forms of knowledge generation that are disadvantaged in traditional research.

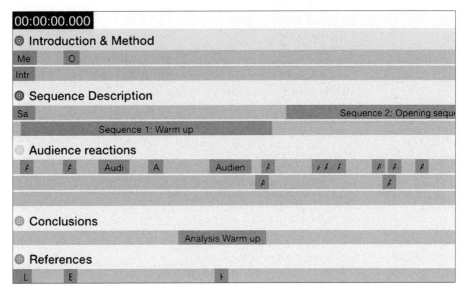

01

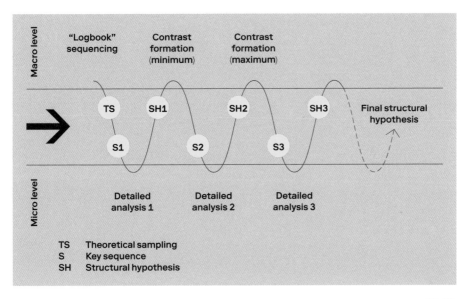

02

Fig. 01:
Emulating the IMRaD model in RV
(illustration by author)

Fig. 02:
Oscillation between macro- and
microanalysis
(illustration by author)

Analytical Method

Macroanalysis	○ Logbook to get an overview of all data material
	○ Description of interesting sequences for "theoretical sampling"
	○ Selection of key sequences
	○ Selection of contrasting sequences (minimum/maximum contrast)
Microanalysis	○ Detailed analysis of selected sequences
	○ Minimum contrast formation
	○ Maximum contrast formation
Formulation of Structural Hypotheses	○ At least three iterations
	○ Final structural hypothesis

This process is not so much falsification but about stren it can be narrated as such.

out verification or

hening perception, and

Structuring the Story:
Audiovisual Storytelling for
Researchers
Martin Zimper

How can a video present the findings of video-based research so that, in terms of structure and format, they comply with the standard rules of a traditional science paper? The following discussion is directed at artistic and applied research in fields such as architecture, design, film, photography, the fine arts, media art, digital art, music, and the performing arts, but the underlying principles can be applied to any kind of academic research.

A traditional science paper usually consists of twenty to forty printed pages. It begins with a title and an abstract and contains up to seven charts and three tables in addition to the main text. It is divided into the sections "Introduction," "Methods," "Results," "Discussion," and "Conclusion." The appendix lists between twenty and fifty additional articles and sources.

No one has defined a video-based format for a first-time scientific publication that can entirely replace the written science paper. With its software tool for annotated videos, the SNSF-funded Research Video project is aiming to make an important contribution to this field. This chapter presents building blocks to help develop the format.

A science paper usually summarizes a one- to four-year research project. The number of filmed minutes in a video, viewed linearly, corresponds to the number of pages in an article. Given the length of a science paper, a duration of twenty to forty-five minutes seems appropriate. This is long enough to go into the necessary detail when presenting the research work, the experiment, and the findings.

Instead of the title introducing a written paper, the video should begin with a title sequence or opening credits that name the lead authors. The title and subtitle can be text-based or animated.

In a research video–as with a paper–this sequence can be followed by an abstract: a short, concise filmic presentation of the project's key findings. Similar to a written abstract, its aim is to stir interest in a serious way and briefly summarize the most important results. From a cinematic perspective, this section resembles a trailer or teaser. It should consist of important highlights of the compiled video material and should last no longer than a minute. Like the synopsis of a film or play, the abstract presents the main findings and structure of the research story in abbreviated form.

The video's actual content should be presented as a dramatic story whose narrative arc is based on traditional dramaturgical structures.

9.1 <u>House</u>: Science as a Dramatic Story

Is not every episode of the hospital series <u>House</u> a type of research video that answers an academic question—specifically, one from the field of diagnostic medicine? Act 1 presents a person who has the symptoms of an unknown disease and thus introduces the problem. In Acts 2 and 3, the team of diagnosticians led by the main character, Dr. Gregory House, uses various methods to diagnose and treat the disease. They repeatedly encounter setbacks or are stymied by false leads. The dramatic climax occurs roughly in the middle of the episode, with the patient fighting for his or her life but ultimately pulling through. In Act 4, a solution is found, the patient is cured, and the medical team gains important new insights. Finally, we see Dr. House in a relaxed social situation. The social order disrupted by the "inciting incident" (the illness) has been restored, and medical knowledge has been expanded.

The same dramatic structure governs court dramas, crime series, and classic detective series such as <u>Sherlock Holmes</u> that follow the rules of the investigation plot. The protagonists are learned intellectuals who uncover a secret or solve a problem and thus restore the disrupted order of the world.

Every episode of <u>House</u> shows the kind of evolutionary process envisioned by Karl Popper, who discussed the ongoing progress of scientific inquiry in his book <u>All Life Is Problem Solving</u>. According to Popper, every theory, even the best, remains valid until it is falsified—that is, refuted. All branches of science exist in their self-created constructs of the world, and, ideally, with each new project, they add a new finding or falsify existing knowledge. A successful project, not only in science but also in artistic and applied research, changes the worldview or story world of a discipline. However, as Gunter Lösel points out in chapter 6, the aim of artistic research is often not falsification or verification, but the strengthening or transformation of perception.

In Christopher Vogler's cinematic concept of a "hero's journey", which draws on the mythological narrative models of Joseph Campbell, the protagonist is first shown in his or her "ordinary world" (that is, everyday surroundings) before being thrust into an unknown special world, in which he or she learns new values, ethical rules, and, in some genres, new physical and natural laws. In this "special world", the protagonist makes friends and enemies and must battle and triumph over an opponent. In Act 3, the protagonist returns to the familiar world and shares his personal reward with the community–a gift, a new sensory perception, acquired knowledge, or a proven strategy.

Applied to research videos, this means that researchers should start by showing their "ordinary world": the daily routine in their discipline, an existing body of verified knowledge, or a defined "subject". In Act 2 they should introduce a new constellation and a "special world".

The principles of action and reaction are foundational not only to drama, but also to science experiments. Scientists subject molecules, substances, bodies, and nature itself to actions and then observe and record their reactions. Artistic research focuses on action, reaction, and interaction–between actors and directors, dancers and choreographers, materials and spaces, and man and machine.

Self-observations by artists or designers during the artistic process combine filmic and inner observations. A research video can portray the emotional and mental worlds of subjects either in audiovisual form through voice-over and shots of people speaking in front of the camera, or abstractly through illustrations, animations, or a combination of live action and motion design.

Artistic research videos can show the artists' dialogue (or confrontation) with themselves and their changed or intensified perceptions of the world. Dialogue, wrote Gustav Freytag, is an essential element of drama: "The most important part of an action has its place in the dialogue scenes, specially scenes between two persons. The purpose of every conversational scene is to bring into prominence from the assertions and counter-assertions, a result which impels the action further."

Freytag goes on to discuss the battle between opposing opinions, between reasons and counter-reasons, evoking the image of "wave-beats"; frequently, he explains, "the third such wave-beat gives the decision." Applied to research videos, this means that a single argument is not enough–at least three are necessary. But Freytag also argues that the plot must constantly move forward. Anything else would be tedious to the viewer. By analogy, research videos should not bore viewers by showing more of the same, but should present variations that imply progress or development.

If a third person appears in the drama, he or she often plays the role of judge or mediator, and structures, evaluates, and integrates what has come before. Perhaps this is exactly what the conclusion of a research video should do: provide an assessment of an entire series of actions and reactions.

Applied to the structure of a research video, we can thus offer the following summary: authors or researchers should begin with a special idea that, in Part 1, they formulate as a hypothesis. In Part 2, they should stage external events in the form of experiments to force their subjects to react. This reaction reveals the subjects' unknown but true nature, which proves or refutes the thesis. The external events (= experiments) are repeated and bolstered at least three times.

9.2   The Acquisition of Knowledge as a Dramatic Turning Point

The most important test and finding should be presented approximately halfway through the video, similar to the climax of a TV series or to what Freytag describes as the "peripeteia" of the classical drama. The term "peripeteia" goes back to Aristotle's Poetics and refers to a sudden turning point that "unties the knot." Although Freytag assigns this climax to the middle of the story, modern screenplay theories tend to see it as part of the third and final act. According to these theories, a "decisive test" should take part in the middle of the drama. Based on this model, researchers could show a decisive test of their scientific or artistic experiment/thesis in the middle of a research video. Is the central idea validated? Does the reaction to an experiment confirm the thesis? Or is it refuted, leading to its demise?

The third part should conclude the series of experiments and tests. If the tests are successful, the solution to the problem or research question should be discussed in detail. This part explores the meaning of the solution for the research community. The resolution should describe the precious "elixir" (a term from Joseph Campbell's mythological narrative models) that the author can pass on to the scientific or artistic community as knowledge.

A research process supported by video can last anywhere from several months to several years. When editing the confrontation phase (second part), the authors should select the results that best exemplify the experiment. In the conclusion (third part), they can formulate the insights they have gained.

9.3 Three Acts According to Hegel: Thesis, Antithesis, Synthesis

The tripartite logic of thesis, antithesis, and synthesis is based on the dialectics of G. F. W. Hegel (1770–1831), who called for and introduced this triadic sequence into the theory of science, thus exerting a profound influence on scientific thinking and writing.

In his book The Art of Scientific Storytelling (2013), the biochemist Rafael E. Luna discusses Freytag's pyramid and the narrative arc of drama and goes on to apply both to scientific writing. His instructions lend themselves well to the format of the annotated research video. Luna's structure can be briefly summarized as follows: In the "Introduction," the author should describe a problem or a major obstacle whose solution or removal will be of great help to humanity.

What Freytag called the "Rising Action" should consist of results and figures—a series of experiments designed and executed to prove and explain the author's introductory hypothesis.

The section "Climax and Peripeteia" (once again Freytag's terms) shows the most important experiment, which conclusively proves the main hypothesis and provides the most compelling evidence of the original hypothesis. The scientific story told by a research video depends on the results of this one experiment. A high degree of dramatic tension results from the circumstances surrounding the experiment, whose outcome cannot be predicted by the previous scientific literature or artistic practice.

According to Luna, "Falling Action with Retarding Elements" should be devoted to further experiments. Because their outcome can be predicted on the basis of findings from the main experiment, they once again validate these findings. The failure of an experiment can also be predicted and additionally confirms the new knowledge.

Luna calls the last section the "Conclusion and Discussion". It should contextualize the new findings within the framework of the scientific discipline. According to Luna, the last paragraph should show that researchers have now completely charted the unknown terrain into which they have ventured with their scientific work or artistic experiments.

The effect of a story in an annotated video depends not only on the structured arrangement of the analyzed processes and data, but also on the videotaped scenes and sequences that are meant to create a dramatic arc. The scenes and images shown in the research video should focus on the results of the experiments and reflect on their fundamental validity and significance in relation to the hypothesis.

How can an annotated research video cite sources published in video format? In the Research Video tool, links can be created to other video sources that are stored outside the actual annotated video. It is important that the platforms are robust and the sources secure so that their existence is guaranteed long after the research video has been published. In our case, the platforms include the Media Archive of the Arts at the Zurich University of the Arts and the Vimeo video portal.

Based on this model, resear test of their scientific or art in the middle of a research validated? Does the reactic confirm the thesis? Or is it re

rs could show a decisive
c experiment/thesis
eo. Is the central idea
o an experiment
ed, leading to its demise?

10

Potentialities:
What's Next for the Research Video Tool
Marisa Godoy

Now what is next? Beyond the developed features of the Research Video tool, what are the Research Video team's dream features still to be realized? What are our suggestions for further investigation of video annotation as the basis for audio-visual publication of research outcomes? What features would have been crucial to make the experience of creating an annotated video article even more effective?

Our discovery-oriented research process to develop Research
Video achieved many aims of the project while giving rise to new
questions and ideas. Due to constraints like timeframe restrictions and technical limitations, not all our visions or wishes emerging from the research process could be realized. What elements
would make the process less laborious? What potentialities are
still to be developed that could facilitate a meaningful experience for the viewer of a Research Video publication?

The Research Video team was comprised of researchers and
practitioners from various fields who explored the Research Video
prototype from different perspectives. Thus the desired but not
yet realized features have likewise been thought through from
different perspectives. This chapter is devoted to outlining our
unfulfilled wishes and our visions for the Research Video tool. We
display the features by listing them according to two perspectives: the creation of a Research Video and the reading-viewing
of a Research Video. We also provide concrete examples as well
as our rationale for including the wished-for features. In order
to offer the reader a clear understanding of each item on the list,
the chapter presents simulated examples in the form of illustrations.

10.1   Creating an Annotated Video Publication
with Research Video

Graphic Annotation

Among other affordances, the use of video material in research
offers the possibility to make visible relationships between various aspects within a given sequence as well as the pointing out
of movement progress and patterns without resorting to textual description. In that regard, graphic annotations such as
tracking of movement trajectories of individuals or objects–high-
lighting gaze cuing of actors and dancers participating in improvisation tasks, for example–can be useful in visually evidenc-
ing an argument presented in text form. In order to draw the
viewer's attention to such video arguments, supporting features
would include the creation of graphic elements on a video sequence (lines, circles, etc.), the option to define the duration of
each graphic, as well as the choice of different colors and the
creation of simultaneous elements on the same sequence.

In the current version, a dot can be added to an annotation to call attention to a specific element in the video, but since the dot cannot follow trajectories, certain types of relationships cannot yet be annotated graphically. Also, more sophisticated graphical annotations like arrows, lines, and circles could be included.

Audio Annotation

In qualitative as well as in artistic research, interviews are a widespread method of data gathering. An audio annotation feature would make possible the inclusion of excerpts from audio data stemming not only from interviews with participants or collaborating artists, but also of audio recordings of creation processes and/or rehearsals. Adding this dimension to the annotated video article, as with the features mentioned above, could grant depth, complexity, and robustness to Research Video publications. In the current version, an audio file can be linked via a URL, but an audio annotation would directly couple the inserted audio to what is being viewed.

User-Defined Track Colors and Hierarchy

When adding tracks to the Timeline, track colors would be ideally chosen by the user. Likewise, when various annotations are created within a single track, the order in which they appear in the timeline would be defined by the user, and not placed by default on top of existing annotations, as is the case in the present version. This would allow for more flexibility in establishing how data is presented or reported, and a more purposeful use of these existing features.

Text Editor and Word Processor

The main type of annotation the Research Video format offers is text-based. Various text editing features such as copy/paste and spell-check (English/UK) are integrated in the tool. Yet other widely used and taken-for-granted text editing features (bold, italics, underline, and so on) offered by most word processors are not possible in Research Video. This means that the degree of complexity that writers working with digital documents are used to is not available. Another feature broadly used in academic publications still to be integrated is the footnote. Footnotes in scholarly publications grant the document a further layer of explanation or clarification, different from what is available in the main text, and helps the author establish various hierarchies of relevance within the text.

Saving and Sharing Files

With regard to the researcher's workflow, the saving of files and the ease of sharing files is one of the aspects of the project that deserves further refinement. Research Video projects must be exported in order to be saved to a hard disk. Ideally, as is the case in existing widely used applications, as soon as a new document is created and saved in the hard drive of the user's choice, a Research Video document would be saved with the known shortcut Command + s.

Currently, sharing files with other people can be done by exporting the file to a commonly accessible drive, or via web applications designed for transferring large files. Preferably, the Research Video document is a stand-alone file that can be easily saved and shared, similarly to text, spreadsheet, and image documents. In the present version, uploading a Research Video file onto the repository or Media Archive of a university is a manifold process for the researcher. The current procedure requires that video and text files be detached from one another before the material can be uploaded.

Personal Sample Project

Depending on the researcher's purposes when creating annotated video files, the creation of various Research Video documents may be necessary. In this kind of situation, it may be essential that tracks must keep the same characteristics (name, color, position below the Timeline). With this feature, it would be possible for the user to generate personal sample projects that contain no annotations but have preestablished characteristics, to which he or she can add new video material, name and export, or save.

Video Editing

The Research Video tool does not have a video editing feature, since developing this function would have been too ambitious for the overall project, and excellent video editing software is available on the market. The audiovisual material must be edited outside Research Video and then imported onto the platform as a video file. However, in data analysis processes for instance, annotation practice is likely to change the annotator's view on the video and changes may be necessary. In an ideal world, video editing would be possible in Research Video so that alterations could be done in the same environment.

Sticky Annotations

In the video editing process, annotations would stay in place whenever parts of the video are cut or edited. This would facilitate the workflow and enable changes to the video material without affecting the coupling of annotations to the timeline. This feature was explored in depth in our subproject Sticky Annotations.

https://docs.google.com/
document/d/1iSm3hNYGaZ9XVQcmHiGYuhSb9p2Eb6XRaSXiLMl3hrY/edit

Embedding Referenced Material

As opposed to making use of hyperlinks or embedding material in the Research Video file, other materials the researcher wants to reference (video, text, and image) could be contained in the Research Video document. This feature potentially safeguards access to referenced files, avoiding unsuccessful access to crucial references due to links that have become inactive or are no longer available online.

Reference Generator

This feature generates a reference caption whenever contents of a Research Video are copied and pasted to another document–a function already operative in some digital books and articles (for example, in the application Books), where the pasted text automatically appears between quotes and includes the author and name of the book, as well as the publisher (see quote below).

"Dance makers have surely, since long ago, left traces that reveal their work intentions and creative processes. Here, we list such traces of process, or materialized intentions, from the broadest point of view: from extended treatises and manifestos to the detail of decision-making and its ordering, movement material in progress (like sketches), as well as analysis when the choreographer looks back and 'discovers' more about intention after a work's completion, explicitly rationalizing what was once intuitive." Excerpt From: Hetty Blades and Emma Meehan, "Performing Process." Apple Books. (Blades and Meehan, 2018: 38).

Subtitles

In the process of reporting data, researchers may consider it essential to present transcripts of audio material. After experimenting with the presentation of audio transcripts in the form of annotations–which appeared in the Inspector component (C) (→ see Chap. 2.2)–it became clear that subtitles would be a more effective feature for providing transcribed audio data.

When creating a Research Video publication, the subtitles have to be generated outside the Research Video tool, namely in a video editing program. The option to convert the annotations to a text that inserts itself as a layer directly on the video itself (subtitle generation) might better the researcher's interaction with audiovisual data while creating an annotated video article, as well as speed up production.

10.2 Viewer's Interaction with a Research Video Publication

A further aspect considered for this chapter relates to the perspective of future users of the Research Video platform: the viewers/readers of annotated video publications. As readers of web-based publications ourselves, we value the possibility to study other researchers' work in depth; hence, our main wishes with regards to the viewers' interaction with the platform relate to making the exploration of a Research Video article a meaningful experience. Reflections on the document's readability and the wish to provide an uncomplicated, smooth exploration of the publication inspired the features listed in this section. Integrating these features could potentially lead to this publication format's ability to reach a wider audience. We gathered experience in navigating existing audiovisual publications and have become increasingly attentive to the need for an accessible yet meaningful engagement with digital materials.

Referentiability

Referencing an annotation in a Research Video is possible by citing the timecode with an additional "a" for annotation (→ see Chap. 7). It would be simpler to reference and share single annotations if each annotation in the Inspector had a Share button, for example, next to the time entry, as illustrated in figure 01.

Also, at any point in the Timeline and for every annotation, an indicator could be generated, a URL address for instance. This indicator, when accessed, would lead the reader directly to the Research Video document online, and to that specific video sequence or annotation. Such a feature would avoid free-floating, unstandardized files and it would also allow the tool to align with academic requirements and long-term standardized procedures that could potentially safeguard the afterlife of documents created in Research Video. Features that support referencing, such as this one, also apply to instances when the author of an annotated video article references her own work when publishing posterior studies (→ fig. 01).

License Declaration

Open access models have an open access license so that documents can be used by a larger community. In that regard, a license declaration would be part of every Research Video file integrated in the interface. As this will usually be some sort of Creative Commons License, the reader-viewer would easily see the conditions for sharing a Research Video.

Key Words, Tags

In the current version of Research Video, tags appear at the end of the text in the Inspector. The viewer needs to search for the tagged word(s) in the whole annotation, which makes it laborious to identify key terms. Preferably, the words corresponding to that tag would automatically be highlighted once the cursor (pointer) is placed on a given tag, similarly to the search tool in a Word document (→ fig. 02).

Further Annotation without Changes to
the Original Document

As we consider the publication of research outcomes in the Research Video format as an alternative to text-based publications, questions emerge as to the degree of interaction with the document possible to viewers for the purposes of their own research. The more the reader can interact with a PDF document, for example, the easier it is to integrate its content into one's own research process and to reference it. Some PDF files allow the reader to copy and paste the text, making the quoting of existing research simple and direct. The question of interaction with a published Research Video document is worth considering if we think about the utility of an annotated video file for other researchers as well as the afterlife of the tool and the publication. In academic contexts, fellow researchers often coauthor articles and conference presentations. This feature would make possible an exchange of interpretations among researchers referencing Research Video articles in their own work. Such possibilities add to the utility and the applicability of the Research Video tool within the arts and research community alike, and potentially to the relevance of its development.

Size of Component Display

All components of the tool, including the Inspector (C), as the annotation field is named, have a fixed size. Preferably, the size of each field could be changed, so these features would allow the viewer to study the annotation material alone by maximizing the component or entering full screen (text-driven exploration), or to study only the video material (video-driven exploration). This kind of navigation would make it possible for the reader to zoom into research data and engage with more detailed, in-depth analysis of annotated video articles.

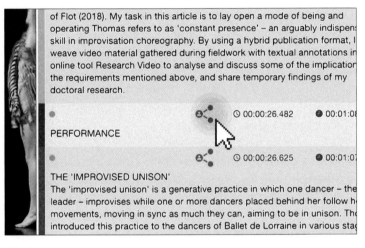

01

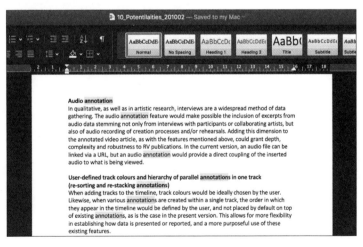

02

Fig. 01:
Example of a Research Video article using a Share button, by Marisa Godoy

Fig. 02:
Highlighted key terms in a Word document

Exporting Different Parts of the Documents

Ideally, various ways of exporting material contained in the published Research Video document would be available. Exports could be image-driven or text-driven. At the moment of export, a dialog box would display checkboxes with options for an image-driven or a text-driven export.

Image-driven exports would constitute a still image of the beginning of an annotation, with the complete correspondent annotations displayed below the image.

In order to export all annotations of a selected track, text-driven exports would display all annotations of that specific track as the primary item in the document. Still images of video data related to that annotation would be displayed on the righthand side.

Hosting of the Research Video Software

Giving all researchers the possibility to easily host the Research Video software on their own (or any arbitrary) webspace would broaden the user base and thus lead to a longer life-span of the tool. In theory, this is already possible since all source code is available on Github; however, at the moment some work is required and possibly only people with the requisite programming expertise might be able to successfully complete the process.

We value the possibility to s
work in depth; hence, our ma
viewers' interaction with the
the exploration of a Researd
experience.

dy other researchers'
wishes with regards to the
atform relate to making
Video article a meaningful

On the Authors

Dr. Gunter Lösel

heads the Research Focus "Performative Practice" at the Zurich University of the Arts, developing models for artistic research in the performing arts. With a background in psychology and in acting, his research interests comprise embodied cognition of acting, collaborative practices, and improvisation. In the SNSF project Research Video he is a principal investigator.

Léa Klaue

is a visual anthropologist and PhD candidate at the Institute of Social Anthropology of the University of Bern; She is also a research associate working on the Research Video project at the Institute for Design Research/Zurich University of the Arts. In her PhD project she conducts research about independent working children in urban Bolivia while using audiovisual ethnographic methods. Her thesis navigates between documentary and fiction short films and anthropological text.

Prof. Dr. Martin Zimper

is Head of "Cast/Audiovisual Media" at Zurich University of the Arts, researching and lecturing on transmedia arts/digital narrative. He is a member of the Academic Steering Committee of Media Technology Center (ETH Zurich) and a lecturer on digital storytelling at the University of St. Gallen (HSG). He is coapplicant in the SNSF project Research Video.

Eric Andreae

studied directing at the University of the Arts in Zurich (ZHdK). Since 2010 he has worked as a research fellow at the university and since 2019 he has been an associate professor in the "Cast/Audiovisual Media" department. In addition, he works as a freelance director for TV and commercial productions. In the Research Video project, he focuses on video production methods.

Martin Grödl & Moritz Resl

founded Process, an experimental design studio based in Vienna that specializes in generative and interactive design and works in the fields of branding, web, installation, and print. As well as traditional graphic design solutions, Process designs and develops highly specialized software that is used as tools for and by clients. In this project they were responsible for concept, design, and development of the Research Video tool.

Marisa Godoy

is a dance researcher, teacher, and award-winning artist based in Zurich. Her creative practice involves stage productions, video installations, and performances in alternative spaces, mostly under the label OONA project, performed in festivals in Switzerland as well as internationally in the UK, France, Germany, South Korea, among others. She is a research associate at Institute for the Performing Arts and Film (IPF)/Zurich University of the Arts (ZHdK), as well as a PhD candidate at C-DaRE/Coventry University.

References

Chapter 1

Elsevier. "Video Articles: Publish, Share and Discover Video Data in Peer-Reviewed, Brief Articles." Accessed July 14, 2020, https://www.elsevier.com/authors/author-resources/research-elements/video-articles.

JER: Journal of Embodied Research. Accessed July 14, 2020, https://jer.openlibhums.org.

JoVE. "About Us." JoVE. Accessed July 14, 2020, https://www.jove.com/about.

Latest Thinking. "About Us." Latest Thinking. Accessed July 14, 2020. https://lt.org/ueber-uns.

Schwab, Michael, and Henk Borgdorff, eds. The Exposition of Artistic Research: Publishing Art in Academia. Leiden, 2014.

Chapter 3

Barbash, Ilisa, and Lucien Taylor. Cross-Cultural Filmmaking: A Handbook for Making Documentary and Ethnographic Films and Videos. Berkeley, 1997.

Chapter 5

Grimshaw, Anna, and Amanda Ravetz. Observational Cinema: Anthropology, Film and the Exploration of Social Life. Bloomington, IN, 2009.

Chapter 6

Derry, Sharon J., Roy D. Pea, Brigid Barron, Randi A. Engle, Frederick Erickson, Ricki Goldman, Rogers Hall, et al. "Conducting Video Research in the Learning Sciences: Guidance on Selection, Analysis, Technology, and Ethics," Journal of the Learning Sciences 19, no. 1 (2010): 3–53, https://doi.org/10.1080/10508400903452884.

Eisewicht, Paul, Pao Nowodworski, Christin Scheurer, and Nico Steinmann. "Seeing Is Believing? Potenziale und Grenzen des vergleichenden Sehens im Video." In Handbuch Qualitative Videoanalyse, edited by Christine Moritz and Corsten, 305–29. Wiesbaden, 2018.

Erickson, F. 2006. "Definition and Analysis of Data from Videotape: Some Research Procedures and Their Rationales." In Handbook of Complementary Methods in Education Research, edited by Judith L. Green, Gregory Camilli, and Patricia B. Elmore, 177–205. Abingdon, UK, 2012.

Geertz, Clifford. "Thick Description: Toward an Interpretive Theory of Culture." In The Interpretation of Cultures, 3rd ed., 3–36. New York, 2017.

Goffman, Erving. Frame Analysis: An Essay on the Organization of Experience. New York, 1974.

Gubrium, Jaber F., and James A. Holstein. The New Language of Qualitative Method. New York, 1997.

Mey, G., and M. Dietrich, "Grounding Visuals Annotationen zur Analyse audiovisueller Daten mit der Grounded-Theory-Methodologie." In Handbuch Qualitative Videoanalyse, edited by Christine Moritz and Michael Corsten, 135–52. Wiesbaden, 2018.

Michel, Burkhard. "Bild- und Videoanalyse in der Dokumentarischen Methode." In Handbuch Qualitative Videoanalyse, edited by Christine Moritz and Michael Corsten. Wiesbaden, 2018.

Moritz, Christine, ed. Transkription von Video- und Filmdaten in der qualitativen Sozialforschung. Annäherungen an einen komplexen Datentypus. Wiesbaden, 2014.

Moritz, Christine, and Michael Corsten, eds. Handbuch Qualitative Videoanalyse. Wiesbaden, 2018.

Ulrich Oevermann, Tilman Allert, Elisabeth Konau, Jürgen Krambeck. "Die Methodologie einer 'objektiven Hermeneutik' und ihre allgemeine forschungslogische Bedeutung in den Sozialwissenschaften." In Interpretative Verfahren in den Sozial- und Textwissenschaften, edited by Hans-Georg Soeffner, 352–434. Metzler, Stuttgart, 1979.

Raab, Jürgen, and Marija Stanisavljevic. "Wissenssoziologische Videohermeneutik." In Handbuch Qualitative Videoanalyse, edited by Christine Moritz and Michael Corsten, 57–71. Wiesbaden, 2018.

Ramey, Kay Ellen, et al. "Qualitative Analysis of Video Data: Standards and Heuristics." In Researchgate. https://www.researchgate.net/publication/319965247_Qualitative_Analysis_of_Video_Data_Standards_and_Heuristics.

Reichertz, Jo. "Die Kunstlehre der wissenssoziologisch-hermeneutischen Videointerpretation." In Handbuch Qualitative Videoanalyse, edited by Christine Moritz and Michael Corsten, 101–17. Wiesbaden, 2018.

Tuma, René. "Video-Interaktionsanalyse zur Feinauswertung von videographisch erhobenen Daten." In Handbuch Qualitative Videoanalyse, edited by Christine Moritz and Michael Corsten, 423–44. Wiesbaden, 2018.

Chapter 8

Glaser, Barney G., and Anselm L. Strauss. Grounded Theory: Strategies for Qualitative Research. Abingdon, UK, 2017.

Chapter 9

Campbell, Joseph. The Hero with a Thousand Faces. Princeton, NJ, 1968.

Freytag, Gustav. Technique of the Drama: An Exposition of Dramatic Composition and Art. New York, 1968.

Luna, Rafael. The Art of Scientific Storytelling. Boston, 2013.

Lupton, Ellen. Design Is Storytelling. New York, 2017.

McKee, Robert. Story: Substance, Structure, Style, and the Principles of Screenwriting. New York, 1997.

Popper, Karl. All Life Is Problem Solving. Abingdon UK, 1999.

Ryan, Marie-Laure, ed. Narrativeacross Media: The Languages of Storytelling. Lincoln, NE, 2004.

Vogler, Christopher. The Writer's Journey: Mythic Structures for Writers, 3rd ed. Studio City, CA, 2007.

Yorke, John. Into the Woods: How Stories Work and Why We Tell Them. London, 2013.

Chapter 10

Blades, Hetty, and Emma Meehan. Introduction to Performing Process: Sharing Dance and Choreographic Practice. 38. Bristol, 2018.

Filming, Researching, Annotating – Research Video Handbook is published to complement the Research Video project (2017-2021), conducted at the Zurich University of the Arts, and funded by the Swiss National Science Foundation.

This book is volume 23 of the subTexte series of the Institute for the Performing Arts and Film, which has provided financial support for its publication.

Unless otherwise noted, all large-format photos are still images taken during the Research Video project. The screenshots depicted in the book were taken directly from the respective programs. The image rights are held by the publishers, if not otherwise indicated at the image.

Research Video Tool developed by Process (https://process.studio)
Direction: Martin Grödl, Moritz Resl
Programmers: Adrian Soluch, Onur Dogangönül
Website Development: Marie Dvorzak

–
Z hdk
–
Zürcher Hochschule der Künste
Zurich University of the Arts
–

Z   hdk
Zürcher Hochschule der Künste
Zurich University of the Arts

Institute for the Performing Arts and Film

SWISS NATIONAL SCIENCE FOUNDATION

Editors:
Gunter Lösel, Martin Zimper

Translation from German into English:
Adam Blauhut (Chapters 3, 8 and 9),
Paul Cohen (Preface and Chapters 4, 5 and 6)

Copy-editing:
Keonaona Peterson

Project management:
Baharak Tajbakhsh, Freya Mohr

Production:
Amelie Solbrig

Layout, cover design, and typesetting:
HE&AD Büro für Gestaltung

Paper:
Magno Natural, 120 g/m²

Printing:
Eberl & Koesel GmbH & Co. KG, Altusried-Krugzell

Image editing:
LVD Gesellschaft für Datenverarbeitung mbH, Berlin

Library of Congress Control Number: 2020952040

Bibliographic information published by the German National Library
The German National Library lists this publication in the Deutsche Nationalbibliografie; detailed bibliographic data are available on the Internet at http://dnb.dnb.de.

ISBN 978-3-0356-2306-2

e-ISBN (PDF) 978-3-0356-2307-9

German Print-ISBN 978-3-0356-2300-0

© 2021 Birkhäuser Verlag GmbH, Basel
P.O. Box 44, 4009 Basel, Switzerland
Part of Walter de Gruyter GmbH, Berlin / Boston

9 8 7 6 5 4 3 2 1
www.birkhauser.com